Praise for *To*

"*Touching Two Worlds* communicates our mysterious human solidarity in pain—the intimate twins of grief and love, two sides of a coin. The author offers a vulnerable and important in-the-moment vocabulary for those of us who are desperate in our grief within the context of our death-phobic society. I can only say thank you for this radical insight."

Jerry White,
corecipient of the 1997 Nobel Peace Prize and
professor of practice, University of Virginia

"*Touching Two Worlds* is a tremendous resource for anyone struggling to find their footing in the aftermath of loss. I've spent my career helping clients heal from trauma and grief, and I'm very grateful to have this book as an important new resource."

Michael Mithoefer, MD
senior medical director for Medical Affairs, Training and
Supervision, MAPS Public Benefit Corporation

"Sherry's deep insights on grief and loss serve as a healing, way-finding journey for so many of us unpacking the complex layers of grief."

Tracey Ivanyshyn
president of UPLevel Global and founder of Good Grief at Work

"From experience, going through grief can be a lonely road, as most don't understand unless they have also experienced it. Dr. Sherry Walling is both a person with that experience and an expert in the subject. I am grateful she has decided to share her wisdom through this book."

Erik Huberman
founder and CEO of Hawke Media

"Dr. Sherry Walling is a psychological rock star who takes you on a cosmic journey of love, death, and grief. Authentic. Bold. Vulnerable. She holds the center. And will help you find yours. Enjoy."

Matt House, DO
president and medical director of House Psychiatric Clinic

"This is an extraordinarily helpful book. It is written by one of the few people that I trust with my mental health. I recommend this to anyone who is confronting a loss or major disruption."

Andrew Warner
founder of Mixergy

"Along with providing tips and strategies throughout the book, the most impactful section is where Sherry promotes kindness and respect to those struggling with their mental health or substance use. Anyone who has lost someone to suicide will find a connection to this book."

Sue Aberholden
executive director of the National Alliance on
Mental Illness (NAMI) Minnesota

"While grief is universal, few of us know how to do it well. In *Touching Two Worlds*, Dr. Walling offers practical, compassionate wisdom to help grieving people (and those who love them) feel less alone in the darkness."

Jordan Harbinger
host of *The Jordan Harbinger Show*

"The reflection and embodiment practices offered here are hard-won, time-tested tools. Dr. Walling speaks directly and openly about real-life, applied strategies that have helped her to continue healing her own heart."

Casey Taft, PhD
staff psychologist, National Center for PTSD, VA Boston Healthcare
System and professor, Boston University School of Medicine

"*Touching Two Worlds* is a gift to be held with both hands, an open heart, and a recognition that we are not alone. As we stumble through a world soaked in pain, Dr. Sherry Walling reminds us that we are not alone. Bound by grief, we are connected in deep and true ways, an accompaniment that we may not have realized we needed but deserve nonetheless."

Erinn Farrell
cofounder and partner of The Coven

"Dr. Walling has written a magnificent guide to grief and grieving. It will surely be a helpful companion to anyone suffering the loss or impending loss of a loved one. Each chapter reads like an opportunity to sit with a friend who deeply understands your pain, and who also has excellent plainspoken advice for getting through all the awful situations that grief puts you through."

Patrick Combs
"Blisspreneur" and master of story

touching two worlds

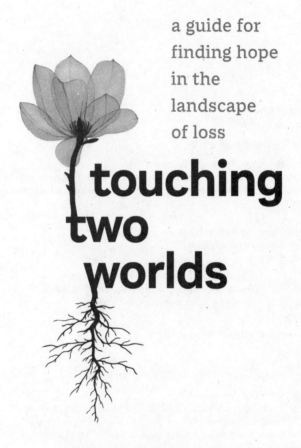

a guide for
finding hope
in the
landscape
of loss

touching
two
worlds

Sherry Walling, PhD

sounds true
BOULDER, COLORADO

Sounds True
Boulder, CO 80306

Published 2022

Cover design by Jennifer Miles
Book design by Karen Polaski

The wood used to produce this book is from
Forest Stewardship Council (FSC) certified forests,
recycled materials, or controlled wood.

Printed in the United States of America

BK06477

Library of Congress Cataloging-in-Publication Data

Names: Walling, Sherry, author.
Title: Touching two worlds : a guide for finding hope in the landscape of
    loss / Sherry Walling.
Description: Boulder, CO : Sounds True, 2022. | Includes bibliographical
    references.
Identifiers: LCCN 2021045094 | ISBN 9781683649670 (paperback) | ISBN
    9781683649687 (ebook)
Subjects: LCSH: Walling, Sherry. | Walling, Sherry--Family. | Children of
    cancer patients--Biography. | Suicide victims--Family
    relationships-Biography | Clinical psychologists-United
    States-Biography. | Grief.
Classification: LCC BF575.G7 W3433 2022 |
    DDC 155.9/37-dc23/eng/20211217
LC record available at https://lccn.loc.gov/2021045094

10 9 8 7 6 5 4 3 2 1

For Tim and Dave.
And for you.
This book is from my broken heart to yours.

Before you know kindness as the deepest thing inside,
you must know sorrow as the other deepest thing.

NAOMI SHIHAB NYE, *KINDNESS*

Contents

Introduction   1

Part One: Two Griefs

Which Aisle for Deathbed Sheets?   7

Can I Have an Armband, Please?   15

Suicide and the Mental Gymnastics of Talking to Kids   19

The Special Art of Crying on Airplanes   25

How to Talk to Grieving People   29

Triggers (and the Unfortunate Loss
   of Perfectly Good Guacamole)   35

Pen in the Wash   39

Disney: Death and Murder for Children   41

Don't Touch Anything (and Bring Music)   47

How to Survive Memorial Services:
   Eat All the Cookies   53

The Emotional Power of Office Supplies   61

Busy Hands and Open Hearts   65

Part Two: Cancer

This Is Not What I Ordered   71

Fight or Surrender?   77

Middle-Class Cancer   85

Touching Two Worlds   89

Fire, Water, and the End of the World   93

Pants Optional   101

Yoga with Dad   105

The Last Day   109

There's a Dead Body in the Living Room   113

The Audacity of the Sunrise   117

Binge-Watching Is My Transitional Object   121
Don't Rush   123

Part Three: Suicide

The Obituary That Was Never Published   129
Dave Is Going to Die   133
Angels in the Zombie Maze   139
Merry-Go-Round of Horrors   147
It Could Be Me   153
When Lifelines Become Entangled   159
The Autopsy in My Inbox   163
The Chapter Where I Grapple
    with Blame and Responsibility   167
Ten Thousand Answers, but No Reason Why   173
I Can't Come with You   177
Death as Light and Feathers   181
You'll Never Know Him   185

Part Four: Life After Death

Metamorphosis   189
Name the Ghosts   191
Heaven: Potluck in the Sky?   197
Fuck It—I'm Joining the Circus   203
I Might Be Too Messed Up to Go to Work   213
Freud Was Right: Death, Sex, and Trauma   217
One Year   221
How Do You Hug a Shadow?   225
Parenting 101: You Must Get Out of Bed   229
Friends Whose Parents Are Alive   233
Public Nudity   237
Too Strong for My Own Good   241
Wait, How Many Kids Do You Have?   247
Sneaky Reemergence of Belief   249
We're All Grieving   255
I'm Okay   257

Afterword   259
Acknowledgments   261
Notes   263
Resources   267
About the Author   269

Introduction

I LOST MY dad and my brother six months apart from each other. Six months to the day. My dad died of esophageal cancer. He was sixty-five. My brother died by suicide. He was thirty-three.

This book is about how those losses reshaped me.

I want you to have fair warning: much of this book is sad. It may invite your own sadness to the surface. This book gives you permission to be sad, to air out the heart's wounds.

If you picked up this book and are reading this introduction, I'm guessing that you have known grief too. Maybe you've lost a parent or a child or a friend or your health or your job. Or maybe someone you love is grieving, and you're trying to understand what's happening to them. Or perhaps you're just a curious mind on a quest to better understand the human condition.

To be honest, I didn't particularly want to write this book. As a clinical psychologist, I'm well practiced at helping people walk through trauma and grief, but I didn't want *this* level of personal expertise. No one does.

Regardless of the specifics, here we are, bound by grief. Co-opted into the least desirable club in which all humans will find themselves at one point or another. Grief is one of the few certainties. My experience is specific—it is about my brother and my father, my children, and me. But much of what I've written here is not at all unique to my family. All of us will lose our parents someday. Most of us will face cancer, some of us will face addiction or mental illness in ourselves or in those we love. All of us will grapple with the universal presence of death.

My deep hope is that this book will help you in your grief, whether it is happening now, lingering in your past, or lurking in the future.

The book is not all sad. It is a little funny, moderately irreverent, and defiantly hopeful. My personal experience of grief is informed by my life as a clinical psychologist, my studies in theology and yoga, and the time I've spent in West Africa and Central America, learning how communities persist in the midst of trauma, genocide, and war.

My personal grief has been accompanied by many moments of feeling wildly lost. I'll confess to fearing that I might not emerge in any recognizable form. Writing has helped me. Reading accounts from others who have carried grief has also helped me. Poetry has helped me. Yoga and aerial arts have helped me. And my professional training has provided me with a sturdy philosophical and practical foundation on which to rebuild my broken heart. I offer those resources to you, in the form of words, given to provide insight, ease, practical tools, and commiseration. There are places in this book where I've written about how my dad and my brother died. In the aftermath of traumatic loss, many people seek out the details, especially what happens to the body of a loved one. "The Last Day" and "There's a Dead Body in the Living Room" especially deal with the physical act of death and dying from cancer. "The Autopsy in My Inbox" shares some details about my brother's suicide. Please know that reading these details may not be wise for you. It may be too much; it may be triggering. Please feel empowered to skip any of the essays or exercises or to put the book aside for a time.

I've written about these details because I long to ease the stigma and hush that surrounds death, especially death by suicide.

I also want to honor the deep attachment that we have to the bodies of our loved ones—which is why many of us long to know the details of what happened to their bodies when they died. I also want to acknowledge that many of us feel that we must hold the details of death in silence. And that silence can lead to misconception, unreal expectation, and stigma. But I do not desire to burden you with images or words that are traumatizing or painful. Please honor your own need to disengage if you feel pulled to stop reading or skip a section.

I've been surprised at how much work grief is. Far more than simple sadness, grief is loud and forceful and dynamic. In this book, I share lots of ideas for things to write, think about, talk about, or do for yourself. Most chapters include a journaling question, grief ritual, meditation, or other practice. My hope is that as you dive in, you'll be accompanied by a few friends or family members who are available for thoughtful, openhearted conversations. It helps to have company. All the questions and writing prompts that I've included in the book can be turned into rich conversations. And some of them may work best within the confines of your own mind and heart—your decision.

Although this book is largely about grief and death, it is also a love story. It is a love story from a daughter to a father and a sister to a brother and a mother to her children. It is the story of how I found little bits of love and wisdom scattered around my life to serve as trail markers to lead me out of the darkest hallows of grief. Sometimes these crumbs were left by my family and friends and sometimes by strangers, authors, and other professionals. And finally, most importantly, it is a love story from me to you. From my broken heart to yours. Although perhaps we've never met, one grieving heart recognizes another, and I honor those tender parts of you just as I've learned to honor them in myself.

I hope that these words will function like a messy, hand-drawn map. There is no precise GPS for getting through grief.

PART ONE

two griefs

Which Aisle for
Deathbed Sheets?

MY DAD DIED on November 10, 2018.

Almost immediately, I began to recite the date. I repeated it over and over in my mind like I was studying it for a high school history test. I was trying to burn the date into my memory: November 10, 2018, November 10, 2018.

My kids listen to this educational song that recounts, in order, the key moments and shifts in recorded civilization. The song is eleven minutes long, and my kids have listened to it so many times that they can now place the Peloponnesian War before India's Mauryan Empire, but after the Olmecs of Mesoamerica. It is quite impressive actually, the number and order of the factoids that they can recite thanks to the "Timeline Song."

Since the day my dad was diagnosed with cancer, my mind has been singing a personal version of a timeline song. The tune is not so catchy, but it has the same function: repeat over and over, and it will become part of your mind.

Repeat it over and over, and it will become reality.

The events of the past few years have been so strange to me that I must force myself to study the story, like something I am learning from the outside in, like something that happened to someone else, and it is important that I get the details right. It is like when I see a new consulting client whose situation is quite complex, I often sit down and create a timeline of the most relevant events. It is a helpful way to get all the facts in order.

I had never needed to use the technique on my own life. Nothing seemed complicated enough to warrant a diagram.

But now, my foggy mind is trying to grasp the events and place them into a logical order so that I can gain some mastery over what has happened.

The basic facts are that my dad is dead, and my brother is dead.

And it all unraveled so very fast.

So that you have a framework for the rest of the story, here is the basic timeline:

> May 28, 1953. My dad was born.
> August 17, 1974. My parents got married.
> September 21, 1978. I arrived. My father became a
> father. I became a daughter.
> June 25, 1982. My brother Dan was born. I became
> a sister.
> May 14, 1985. My brother Dave was born.

(A bunch of stuff happened—my brothers and I grew up and made our lives. I married a man named Rob, built a career, became a mother, did some traveling, adopted a pet turtle from Craigslist, and watched a bit of Netflix.)

Here is the newer history, the part I am trying to memorize:

> February 3, 2017. A mass was found in my
> dad's esophagus.
> February 16, 2017. We received a phone call that
> my brother Dave was in the ICU in Kalispell,
> Montana. He was almost dead.
> March 1, 2017. We learned that my dad's cancer was
> in his esophagus, lymph nodes, and right lung.

March 17, 2017. Dave entered his first
course of treatment for alcohol addiction
and depression.

September 2017. Cancer spread to my dad's liver.

May 2018. Cancer spread to my dad's brain.

June 2018. Dave lost his sobriety and spent the
summer in and out of the hospital.

November 10, 2018. My dad died.

January 20, 2019. Dave very nearly died of self-
inflicted injuries.

April 26, 2019. Dave completed treatment and
decided to return to Montana.

May 10, 2019. Dave died.

En route to finishing my PhD in clinical psychology, I did a training year administering neuropsychological assessments at a brain injury recovery center in Southern California.

Every day I asked my patients for four simple pieces of information:

Please tell me your name.
What is the date today?
Please tell me where you are.
Why are you here?

We also ask versions of these questions in the psychiatric emergency room.

The answers to these questions reveal someone's mental state, their orientation to place and time.

Does someone know *who* they are, *where* they are, *when* they are, and *why* they are there?

Those are the basics. You are supposed to know that information at all times.

When my patients answered those questions accurately, I wrote a little note in their chart: "Oriented x4." When they couldn't answer those questions, the note was much longer. Lack of orientation signifies an issue, a big issue. It is a bad sign when someone doesn't know where, who, why, or when about their own present context. It means more tests and assessments, increased observation from the other clinical staff, and a consultation with the attending physician.

I repeat the dates in my mind. Placing my days in the timeline of these deaths. Making sure I'm oriented. Reorienting when I'm not clear on who or where or when or why.

Three days before my dad died, I was at Target, buying sheets for the extra-long twin bed that the hospice team had placed in my parent's living room. I walked around the store in a daze. I couldn't quite grasp why I was there. Why I needed new sheets for a strangely shaped bed. The last time I bought sheets this size was when I moved into a college dorm. Those are the only two uses for the extra-long twin bed: dorm rooms and deathbeds. Isn't that so strange?

I couldn't find what I needed, but I didn't want to ask the Target people for help. I was afraid of explaining about the sheets and why I needed the unusual size. That was back when I actively avoided crying in public.

It is a lot of pressure to buy deathbed sheets. I looked for the softest ones. I debated the colors. Gray sheets matched my mood, but would they make his complexation look more death-like? Wouldn't that be creepy? Like he was being swallowed into gray and transforming into a skeleton or a tombstone.

Yellow sheets seemed out of place and stupidly cheerful for the occasion of dying. I imagined yellow sheets in a country-style bed-and-breakfast. There should be a mason jar of sunflowers and a brightly colored quilt. Perhaps the scent of freshly baked cookies. No, yellow wasn't right.

White felt too hospital-like for a die-at-home-in-the-living-room scenario. I smelled bleach just looking at the package.

Sage green was too close to gray. Too much like vomit, and gangrene, and zombies.

I went with light blue. Blue seemed like the safest bet. Sky-colored. Heavenly.

Orientation check: My name is Sherry. I am Tim's daughter. It is November 6, 2018. I am in Target. I am buying sheets for the bed where my dad will die. He will die very soon.

Whew, I am oriented. I know where I am and why I'm there. I know my name. I know the date. Check, check, check. Oriented x4.

You have to say the dates over and over because death is so disorienting.

Tuesday, April 25, 2019. I was packing to go on a fabulous trip with a group of women entrepreneurs. I called my brother on the phone to see if I could stop by and see him on my way to the airport. He wasn't home. He was at a doctor's appointment across town. "Shoot," I said, "I wish I could give you a hug." He was getting on a train to move back to Montana. He was supposed to go on May 6, but he moved up the date, and it was during my trip so I wouldn't have the chance to see him in person before he left. For two years, we'd lived in the same city. But the mountains were calling his wild soul, so he made plans to return to Glacier National Park, the place he most loved in the world. He was newly sober, newly recovering from crisis. He was hopeful. He sounded years younger than he had six months ago. He sounded grounded. He sounded happy.

I didn't get to hug him good-bye.

But I did tell him that I loved him. That was the last thing I said to him before he died: *I love you.*

Orientation check: My name is Sherry. I am Dave's sister. It is May 10, 2019. I am sitting in the dirt in my backyard. I am crying because my brother died. I am crying because I loved him.

I am oriented. I know where I am and why I'm there. I know my name. I know the date. Check, check, check. Oriented x4.

The thing about death is that it rewrites everything. That is why you have to practice the dates. The date goes on the tombstone and on the obituary and on all the paperwork and on Wikipedia, so you have to remember it properly, you have to get it right.

Death also rewrites the story of the living. It shifts those of us left behind. The child who can no longer say "my parents." Because one of them is gone. The parent who struggles to explain how many children they have after one passes away. The simple details with which we introduce ourselves, the basic specifications of our lives, are altered by death.

I used to be a daughter with a dad. A dad that texted me photos of his perfectly barbequed ribs and selfies that he took with his golden retriever. No one texts me barbeque photos anymore.

When people ask about my family, I've started saying, "My mom lives in Redding, California," instead of, "My parents . . ." He's been edited out of my personal introduction.

And I used to say that I have two younger brothers. And now that I have one, I say, "I have a brother that lives in Sacramento. And a brother that passed away."

It takes a lot of mental work to remember that. I have to write it down and study it.

I'm trying to reorient to this new timeline, this new history. But the truth is that I am resisting it, I'm not being a good student because I don't really like the story. It feels like a bad dream that I might someday wake from. I'm working against myself because I don't want it to be true. I don't like this story at all.

Yet, it is now my story. I have to learn the dates. I have to discipline my mind and force myself to absorb the information that I'd rather not know. It is hard work. But I know that it is important work if I want to find a new wholeness as I walk through the rest of my timeline.

take a moment . . .

Take a moment to write down the timeline of your grief. Find a blank piece of paper; get out your calendar. Note down the significant dates and times of the events that led you to this moment.

Maybe your timeline will begin with a phone call, maybe it will begin with the day they were born. Maybe it will begin with one drink.

List the events in the order that they occurred.

Your timeline may span ten years or two hours. Regardless of the duration, it is helpful to make concrete the key steps in your story. This moves the experience out of the circling hamster wheel in your mind and onto the black and white of a blank page. The practice begins to give you mastery over the "facts of the story" and helps the details feel accessible rather than overwhelming or foggy. Writing emotionally charged content in a structured way allows your brain to engage the material in a diversified manner—you use different centers of the brain when you write than when you speak or cry. You experience less emotional fatigue when you change the mode of communication or the emotional tone of the expression.

After you write it down, take a moment to absorb all that has transpired to lead you to this moment of grief.

Take a moment to honor all that you've walked through.

Can I Have an Armband, Please?

I WISH WE still wore black following the death of a family member.

In many traditional societies, members of the immediate family wore black for up to two years after the death of a loved one. Apparently, the tradition of wearing black dates back to the Roman Empire. Different ethnic groups have a different color for mourning: white in China, black and red in Ghana, purple among some Catholic communities in Latin America.

It is a classy way to let the world know: My heart is broken. Don't fuck with me.

It is a cruel by-product of a modern, connected society that bereaved people are expected to roll right on with their lives after a loved one passes away. My brother Dan got two days of bereavement leave when our dad died. Because I work for myself, I took as many days as I wanted, so long as I wasn't concerned about a paycheck. I took about ten days off before he died and a handful of days after he died.

Death didn't stop me from getting way behind on email. I got weeks behind. The school librarian was out for blood because one of my kids misplaced a book called *Dog Man*. Someone sent me a contract, and it took me two weeks to respond when it would normally take six hours. It was a speaking gig I really wanted, but I let it sit there in my inbox and couldn't seem to find the energy to deal with it. At one point, my inbox also contained an email from the sheriff's assistant. My brother's autopsy report was right there as a pdf.

The autopsy came in right under the chastising note from the librarian.

I'm in constant awe at how life keeps marching on. There are groceries and dishes. And playdates. My hair needs to be washed. The children need to be fed. My career needs to be tended to.

Mostly I kept moving, functioning, managing the tasks, but sometimes I started crying in the middle of my life. It happened out of the blue. In Trader Joe's. In yoga class. It almost always happened when I was on an airplane.

If I were wearing black, it wouldn't seem so very strange. There would be a built-in explanation instead of the wide-eyed, concerned shock of strangers.

If I were wearing black, people would understand why I'm slow to laugh, why I sometimes look dazed, why I feel dazed.

If I were wearing black on my social media pages, people would be gentler with their comments.

If I were wearing black, it would reveal the reason why the world around me doesn't always feel like home.

If I were wearing black, people would know that part of my heart is somewhere else. In the shadowlands. In the cold, dark places. A part of me is among the dead.

Two years of mourning clothes. That tells the world that this span of time is different from the time before it or the time after it. This time is set aside. It is the time to be quiet and reflective. It is earmarked for memory and wish and regret and tears and longing and days in bed and simple sadness.

And also, complex sadness. The kind of sadness that includes anger, guilt, fear, and sleeplessness. There should be an extra black band for those bereaved by suicide. That's a different deal—there are some extra stages of grieving to work through.

The black mourning cloth on my body would coordinate with the circles under my eyes.

It would tell the world that this span of time does not include timely responses to email.

It does not include deep concern for misplaced library books.

take a moment . . .

Take a moment to make a list of people who need to know that grief has caused a disruption in your life. I know you don't *want* that to be the case. I know you don't want to be disrupted.

But I promise, it will be easier for you (and for those you love) if the key people in your life know that you're coping with a loss. This exercise also serves as a reminder that the effects of a crisis are not held by you alone—they emanate to those around you, like a drop of water in a still pool.

The list will likely include people like your employer and close professional contacts, your close friends, your children's teachers, anybody with whom you are in the middle of a big project (like a kitchen remodel, building a website, a writing project), your family members, and the family members of your significant other.

These people are your grief team. They are your tribe and the ones who will walk through this with you. Don't be afraid to ask for help or support (as appropriate to their role in your life).

Your message can be informal, but it should be as specific as possible about the disruption that grief may cause.

An example for a colleague: "I've recently lost my mother. I am going to take a few days off and will then work part-time for a week or so. I may be slower to respond to email than normal. I continue to be very excited about the work we're doing together, so please don't interpret my slowness as a lack of enthusiasm. I'm finding that I need some extra time to grieve and spend time with my family."

We don't have armbands anymore. But that doesn't mean that we have to keep moving as if nothing has happened. If you ask for

the space that you need, most reasonable people will respond
with kindness and flexibility. Many people don't recognize the need
for space and aren't respectful enough of their own grief to dare
to ask.

Suicide and the
Mental Gymnastics
of Talking to Kids

I HAVE THREE children. During the season of these deaths, they were twelve, eight, and eight. They are tender and sweet. And young. But also old enough.

The kids knew all about cancer. After my dad's initial diagnosis, he and my mom and Rosy the golden retriever drove from California to Minnesota to stay with our family while my dad did an evaluation and treatment plan at the Mayo Clinic. They stayed for two months. There was a lot of talk about cancer at our house. The kids knew the science. They shared a house with my dad while he went through his first round of chemo. They knew it was miserable. They knew he was sick.

Early on I let them know that this cancer would probably cause Grandpa to die. I explained the size and location of the various tumors. I let them know that our time with him would probably be two or three years.

I believe in being honest with children. Honest in a way that they can understand.

I didn't want them to be afraid that Grandpa would die. I wanted to let them in on the secret that Grandpa *was* going to die. No need to keep anyone in suspense.

I was with my dad when he died in California. My children were at home in Minnesota. A few minutes after he died, I called them on the phone. My husband, Rob, sat with them, and I told them one by one. I talked to them while Rob held them. My oldest son wailed. He cried with his whole body. At full volume. I almost dropped my phone, it made me feel so sick.

I never want to hear that sound again.

The younger two were quieter. Timid. Tender. Sad. Scared.

How I wished to hold them and let them feel my strong, alive arms. To let them know that, although my dad had died, their mother would never die. Never. I wouldn't do that to them. Ever.

How I wished for that.

When my brother died, Rob and I both sat with the children. We told the youngest and the oldest together. They were once again tender and fearful. Surprised. Wide eyed. We held them. They didn't say much. Uncharacteristically, they didn't ask any questions. They knew that Uncle Dave was mysteriously sick. I suppose something in them knew not to ask for lots of details.

When he heard the news about Uncle Dave, my middle child collapsed and sobbed. He melted into Rob's arms. He started crying and didn't stop for a long time. His eyes were sad and scared, and he cried giant elephant tears that seemed to come from the core of his being. I carried him upstairs, and he lay in my bed with his head resting on my belly. He cried himself to sleep that night. He cried a lot in the days that followed.

He still cries about it sometimes.

My brother's death was much more difficult to talk about with my children. They knew that he struggled with alcohol. They knew the word *addiction*. They knew that he had been in and out of the hospital.

They also knew him well. When he was sober, he was at our house almost daily: doing laundry, borrowing a paddleboard, helping with dinner. He played baseball with them. He tossed the Frisbee and made popcorn for movies.

Of all our extended family, he is the one they'd spent the most time with. He was the one who was woven into their lives.

What to say? How to help them understand this story?

Simple and true: "Uncle Dave was having a very hard time, and he was drinking too much alcohol. The drinking made him really sick and damaged the cells in his brain. He tried hard to get better. He wasn't able to get better. He died."

That is what I told them. Something like that.

The problem with suicide is that there's no good way to make the logic work for children.

I can describe cancer to my kids. "Something goes wrong in the DNA of the cells so that they start reproducing very fast. These new cells are dense, and they become tumors that clog the other areas of the body. And those clogging tumors damage the insides so that they no longer work correctly." This explanation isn't perfect, but it gets the job done. It makes sense. You can visualize it. Demonstrate it with crayons on paper if you need to.

> He couldn't find a way out.
> He didn't want to live anymore.
> He was too sad.
> He ended his life.
> He stood in front of a train.

Those are things that I can't explain very well.

And it isn't logic that I want them to understand. I don't want them to nod their heads and say, "Okay, I get it. When people get very sad and hopeless, they end their lives to ease their suffering."

I can just imagine the torrent of questions: How much sadness is too much sadness? How much pain is too much pain? When the cat dies? When my best friend is mad at me? What makes your heart hurt so much that dying is the logical step? When does one reach that point?

Never. Never, children! Never. Never. Never. That is what your mother says.

One of my consulting clients once said to me, "I hate when people talk about all the good things about someone who has died by suicide. When people idolize them, they ignore the fact that they've committed murder."

Murder. Hmm, that doesn't quite work either.

Dave was loving and kind. Not a murderous bone in his body. I can't villainize him or write him off as some ridiculous, out-to-lunch person. "Only crazy people kill themselves. Only really sick people kill themselves. Suicide is selfish. Suicide is murder." Dave wasn't crazy. My children knew him. I can't lie to them about who he was in order to scare them away from something I never want them to have any awareness of.

Psychologically speaking, talking with my children about Dave's death was so hard because it threatened to dismantle their basic assumptions about the goodness, safety, and predictability of the world. Whether we're aware of it or not, most of us walk around with a default belief that generally falls in line with the just-world hypothesis: Good things happen to good people, and bad things happen to bad people. We start out with this philosophy as our factory setting.

In her book *Shattered Assumptions*, Ronnie Janoff-Bulman[1] expands on the just-world hypothesis to identify three assumptions that are particularly vulnerable in the face of trauma or loss: *The world is benevolent. The world is meaningful. The self is worthy.*

In my conversation with my children, I didn't want their sense of goodness, justice, and safety to be shattered. The world is no longer a predictable, good place when someone kind and loving experiences such darkness and ultimately a horrible, self-inflicted death. The world is no longer meaningful when there is no simple, rational explanation for how such a thing happened. The self may no longer be worthy of happiness and joy if someone like Uncle Dave could not find happiness and joy.

Everything in me is organized against my children understanding this logic. I didn't want it to enter their minds or their hearts.

But it has. It will. They will come to know the full story of their soft-spoken uncle with the beautiful blue eyes. They will remember him on our couch and in the park and in the kitchen and at the lake. They will know the truth about him and how he was lost. And there is no way around the reality of suicide, the reality that the truth is beyond the careful, thoughtful, simple explanations of their mother. I can't make it neat or easily digestible for them. It is too messy.

take a moment . . .

The cognitive work required to recover from trauma involves rewriting the default assumptions to accommodate, or make room for, the reality of the terrible thing that has happened. Sometimes this is as simple as softening the default assumptions:

> The world is benevolent.

> The world is meaningful.

> The self is worthy.

These can be rephrased to be more accurate:

> The world can be benevolent but is not guaranteed to be fair.

> The world is *often* meaningful, but sometimes meaning eludes us in the moment.

> The self *is* worthy but also vulnerable to tragedy and mistreatment beyond our control.

Take a moment to write down the assumptions that have shifted within you as a result of your loss.

Your assumptions may come from your childhood beliefs:

> *My dad always takes care of me.*

They may be default beliefs about society:

>   *Doctors are competent and trustworthy.*

They may be existential beliefs:

>   *God doesn't give us more than we can handle.*

Write down four to five that come to mind.

Next, try to see if you can rewrite the basic beliefs in a way that creates space for the loss that you've experienced. See if you can stretch the assumption rather than let it shatter.

Here are some examples:

DEFAULT ASSUMPTION	REVISED ASSUMPTION
My dad always takes care of me.	My dad took excellent care of me when I was a child. That was his deep joy and most important job. I am an adult now and I can care for myself.
Doctors are competent and trustworthy.	Doctors are usually competent and trustworthy. But they are human, and sometimes they make mistakes.
God doesn't give us more than we can handle.	I believe that God is loving and present. But I don't always understand what God is doing.
Suicide is a sin.	Suicide is complex and painful. Sometimes wonderful, loving people end their lives by suicide.

When you notice yourself stuck on a part of your grief that seems like a basic belief or fundamental assumption, write it down. See if you can rewrite it and make it work. If you can't, perhaps consider whether or not that belief really works for you. Perhaps it is one that you can release to the wind.

The Special Art of Crying on Airplanes

I'VE PERFECTED THE art of crying on an airplane.

Two days after Dave died, I flew from Atlanta to Punta Cana in the Dominican Republic. I was on my way to facilitate a corporate retreat, an event that I'd been carefully planning for three months. Perhaps it was not the best choice to stick with my professional plans, but at the moment I welcomed the distraction.

I cried the entire flight. Three hours. In an act of great mercy, I was upgraded to a window seat in first class. I could huddle toward the wall and keep my tears more or less to myself. I was in a big seat, so there were a few more inches between me and the stranger next to me. My seatmate was either drunk or sleep deprived or both—either way she was one notch above comatose and absolutely unconcerned with me.

Oddly, I sat by her again five days later on my return flight. She recognized me. Perhaps I should give her more credit. Perhaps she was compassionately pretending not to notice the fact that I was an utter mess on a first-class flight to paradise. She couldn't know that my baby brother's body had just been recovered from a field in northern Montana.

Air travel has been a big part of my life during all this. When my dad was diagnosed with cancer, I decided that I would go see him every three months. It was a lot of trips.

Sometimes I went with the kids, mostly I went by myself. Visiting him that often was one of my best decisions. I flew from Minneapolis, where I live, to Sacramento, the closest airport to my parents' house, at least fifteen times in the span between my dad's diagnosis and his memorial service.

I have it down to a perfectly efficient system. There's a Thursday-evening direct flight on Delta. I never check a bag. I step off the plane and walk to the rental car shuttle. I rent with Hertz, and I have gold status, so I choose the car that I want without stopping at the desk. If the kids are with me, I let them pick the car. They always choose based on color: red or blue. Once they chose a bright-red jeep, which was fun in principle, but the plastic roof rattled a lot flying up Interstate 5. I leave the airport, drive twenty minutes north to Woodland to stop at In-N-Out. I use the drive-through and nourish my inner Californian with a Double-Double in a brown box. And fries. And a vanilla milkshake if I'm feeling particularly decadent. I drive the two hours north to my parents' home in Redding. All these steps choreographed with the efficiency and grace of a business traveler.

However, when I'm on a plane and I have to be still, the grace and efficiency disappears. When there are limited things to occupy my mind, I do a lot of thinking. And writing.

And crying.

The truth is I cry all the time on airplanes now. Since February 2017, I can't remember a single tearless flight.

I used to visit casually with my seatmates and then eventually put on my headphones to do some work or watch a movie. I exchanged business cards, networked, got restaurant recommendations. I made new friends and learned new things. I kept up with the new movies. I was a fully functional grown-up with graceful social skills.

I don't speak to anyone now. I know it is coming. There's too much stillness and too many grief associations for me to get through a flight without some tears shed.

Most of this book was written through tears from the window seat.

I'm a huge fan of the window seat. It affords the most privacy.

I'm also a huge fan of wearing a hoodie. I'm a grown-up professional with three kids and a nice car, but I have been known to pull the hood of a sweatshirt almost over my eyes as the ultimate act of "Please, don't talk to me."

And thank goodness for earbuds.

I know that people can see me crying. The flight attendants are extra tender to me when they ask what I'd like to drink. Usually they give me two bags of Cheez-Its or two little bottles of gin instead of one.

One woman who sat in the middle seat was reading over my shoulder as I wrote the section of this book about receiving Dave's autopsy. She looked at me for a long time. I suppose, contemplating what kind, comforting thing she might say. In the end, she didn't say anything.

That is fine with me.

Being in grief on a plane is to be having an intensely personal experience in the midst of complete strangers. It is both excruciatingly uncomfortable and strangely comforting.

I like that I am not alone, and I don't feel any need to explain myself. On the plane, in the window seat, I don't have to try to hide my tears from my children or try to convince them that Mommy is really okay. I don't have to see my husband's gentle disappointment that, yes, I'm crying again. Yes, I'm still sad. Yes, I've failed to remember to unload the dishwasher or order the gluten-free bread.

The strangers don't care. So long as I stay away from sobs or ugly cries, so long as there's no snot, they are content to honor the gentle stream of tears with dignified denial. They're not disappointed or dysregulated. They're tender or avoidant—both work for me. I suppose they assume that there's a good reason for my emotional unrest, and they leave me alone.

And I love them for that.

take a moment . . .

Get a soft hoodie and some big sunglasses. Throw them in your
bag along with a packet of tissues.

Just in case.

It sounds like I'm being glib, but I'm completely serious. It is
psychologically important to have a strategy for how to cope in
the moments when the grief spills over. Maybe you're not prone to
tears, and maybe you're not spending time on airplanes, but being
in grief means that you have less emotional reserve than normal,
less patience, less social creativity. You may be tearful. You may be
irritable and more likely to snap at the others. You may be inclined
to withdraw into online shopping or Instagram or some other self-
soothing, mild dissociation.

It is helpful to think through what physical comfort measures
might be important to have on hand during the moments of
intense grief.

I like a hoodie because it surrounds my head and gives me
privacy and a sense of being enclosed, like a hug for my head.
Wearing a hood on a plane also sends a strong signal that I'm not
open for engagement. It might be the closest thing to a mourning
armband available.

Perhaps your chosen object is a special scarf that protects and
barricades your neck in the moments when it is hard to breathe or
the sadness threatens to close your throat. Perhaps a baseball hat
that can cover tears for a moment when you look down. Perhaps
you invest in some big headphones that cover your ears and block
out the swirling sounds of the loud world around you. Perhaps
you select a soft, heavy blanket that you crawl under late in the
afternoon when you're tired and out of patience with the kids, and
your grief is becoming very heavy.

It is helpful to have a resource, a designated physical object that is
comforting and affords you a level of emotional protection from the
overwhelmingness of the world around you and the grief within you.

How to Talk to Grieving People

I SPENT MY junior year of college living in West Africa.

When I returned from my year away, my friends would ask, "How was it?" And I would stare at them awkwardly. My blank response was not because I didn't want to share but because it was so hard to know where to start.

The really good stories required a lot of background—like what a *tro tro* is, why you never touch anyone with your left hand, and how toilets aren't toilets at all but a small drain in a concrete floor.

It was so different that it was hard to explain. Every taste, every scent, every shade of green. The way of saying hello. The way of being a friend. The scent of the rain. The color of the dirt. Every detail of life was new and fresh and foreign and a little disorienting. While there, I carried a five-gallon bucket of water on my head each morning and then used a pump to purify the day's drinking water. There was no hot water. The electricity worked only sometimes. My university friends shared a handful of books for forty students in a class and memorized the teacher's notes verbatim. Every morning I had to check my shoes for scorpions and terrible spiders. All of that was normal—it became part of the rhythm of my life.

Over the course of the year, I accumulated so many stories that it is difficult to know where to start or to capture the essence of my experience without a really long conversation. There was the time that I was bitten by a monkey. The time that I hitchhiked to the border of Ghana and Burkina Faso. The time my lab partner asked me to marry him and really meant it. The time I mistakenly urinated in someone's bathing area because I asked for the bathroom and not the toilet, and toilets aren't toilets anyway, so it can be very confusing. It is impossible to tell these stories in a sentence or even a paragraph.

To sum up my experience with "great" or "fine" made my heart hurt. It reduced something so immense and meaningful to a sound bite. I'd almost rather keep it to myself than try to cram the immensity into a few words to satisfy someone's casual interest.

One of the great heartaches of grief is how hard it is to explain to people, especially the people that I love.

When people find out that my brother died, they look at me with wide eyes and say, "I'm so sorry . . . How are you?" I fumble through some lame version of "I'm okay," and we change the subject and move on. Some friends never bring it up again.

The real answer is, "My whole world is different. A million things are different. All the assumptions have changed. All the colors are different." But I can't explain all that without some follow-up questions. And time. It is a long, one-sided conversation.

The one-and-done "How are you?" conversation is bullshit.

Grief is very isolating. It is isolating for the bereaved and for those that love them.

It is a years-long solitary journey to a distant land. And communication is hard.

I lived in West Africa from 1998 to 1999. The internet was just catching on. No one had cell phones. No one had personal computers. I was dating Rob at the time, and we wrote letters back and forth—letters that took weeks to arrive and were outdated

bear to form the words in my mouth. That would make them real. It was easier to be quiet. The people that I did tell seemed shocked and sad, and I felt pulled to tend to their feelings. I felt more and more isolated. The more isolated I felt, the harder it became to talk about it. It became a cycle of silence.

Unfortunately, there were also a number of occasions when people said really unhelpful things. One of the harder comments that someone said to me about Dave's death was, "Well, you kind of knew that this would happen." And while that's objectively true, it felt so unhelpful to my grief because, yes, in my thinking brain, I knew it may happen, but my brother still died in a shocking and violent way. And I am absolutely destroyed by it. Give me a little space to fall apart before pointing out all the ways that this was predictable and that I should have had time to prepare emotionally. The knowing that the thing is going to happen doesn't eliminate the grief. I knew my father was going to die of cancer, and I was still in grief. The psychologist part of my brain could predict that Dave would probably die early and that suicide may be the cause, but that doesn't negate the mountain of pain I now sit with. Loving friends don't always know what to say or what to ask.

When I came back from Africa, I didn't need to share all my wild stories with everyone in my life. But it was important to me that they somehow acknowledged that I had been somewhere different and that it had changed me. Grief has felt very similar. We cannot pretend that life is the way it used to be or that I am the way I used to be. That is not a sustainable assumption.

I find the most solace with friends who have lost parents or other loved ones. There's a shared experience without speaking. I don't have to explain how I'm feeling or why I can't sleep at night or why I'm desperate to tell someone a story about the time when, as children, my brothers and I found a discarded stop sign, and we risked life and limb to transport it in a wagon back to our house, feeling that we'd cheated death and conquered the world. We hung it in our tree fort where it stood as a totem to our shared mischief and willingness to work together to acquire treasures that may or may not have been procured in violation of some local law. Those precious memories are delightful, but sometimes they burn inside of me.

People who've known loss understand the tension between wanting to talk endlessly about the memories and the need to remain in sealed quiet.

take a moment . . .

If you'll permit me, here are a few suggestions for how to care for grieving people.

- Send them something. Because loss is the absence of something, the presence of things feels oddly helpful. Flowers. A card. My friend Carey sent great care packages with nail polish and chocolate bars. My friend Brooke sent a simple seashell necklace. My friend Theresa had a bouquet made from flowers that grow near Glacier National Park in Montana. Holding the tangible thing helps counterbalance the untethered feeling that goes along with reaching out for somebody who used to be there and isn't there anymore. My mother sends photos through the mail. Sending something expresses love when a long conversation is difficult.

- Help with the practical stuff. There are so many practical things that go along with loss. The logistics are a nightmare—lots of paperwork and phone calls. Grief leaves many of us not deeply interested in daily things, like cooking. One friend sent gift cards for Uber Eats. Other friends have sent gift certificates to local restaurants. After my dad died, the ladies in my mom's Bible study loaded her fridge and freezer so that she didn't have to cook for months if she didn't want to. One friend came over to help with her yard work.

- Ask about the person that died. My friend Jamie once asked, "Do you want to tell me a story about Dave?" That is the best question to ask any grieving person. He's on my mind constantly. And it is killing me that he's gone and that the world will miss the opportunity to know him. So, when someone invites me to talk about him, it is a huge gift. It moves him from the shadows into the present tense. It makes him a tiny bit alive, because he's the subject of a real conversation.

- Rephrase "How are you?" into something more specific. How are the holidays feeling this year? What most reminds you of your grandmother? How are you sleeping these days? Is anything making you laugh right now? What has surprised you about the way you feel after the loss of your sister? Asking about a specific part of someone's well-being helps focus the conversation and prevents overwhelm. It also conveys caring and interest.

- I've also found it really helpful when people have said, "I don't know what to say. But I love you, and I have two hours absolutely free to talk, or take a walk, or do anything that you'd like." A friend who didn't know what to say made me a playlist on Spotify. It was made up of songs that helped her feel grounded when she was sad. It was a beautiful, soulful gift from her heart to mine.

If you are in grief and any of these suggestions sound good to you, go back to your list of people, the list you made a few chapters ago, and let a few of those people know about these helpful tips. Let them know how they can best support you right now. Don't assume that they know the best way to show up. If you can muster the energy, let them know what you need.

Triggers

*(and the Unfortunate Loss of
Perfectly Good Guacamole)*

I WAS MUNCHING on nachos with extra guacamole at a Mexican restaurant when one of my luncheon friends started talking about his experience battling cancer ten years earlier. He told us about his symptoms and eventual diagnosis. He described what it had been like for his wife and children.

He was beginning to explain how miserable chemo made him feel when I had to abandon my nachos and excuse myself to hide out in the bathroom for ten minutes. I couldn't listen anymore.

How shitty is that?

He was authentically reflecting on a powerful personal experience around a table of friends. He was telling his story. It was a supernormal friend conversation, one that was vulnerable and tender, the kind of conversation that I deeply value.

But I just couldn't sit and listen. I couldn't be a curious, compassionate friend in that moment.

The air left my lungs. The conversation brought back waves of memories of my dad vomiting in our guest bathroom. I could hear the retching as my friend talked. I imagined my dad wrapping himself in layers and layers of clothes to fight the chills. I suddenly felt hot and like I couldn't breathe.

Chemo is terrible.

My friend sharing his experience triggered me. In therapy we talk about the word *trigger* as something you unexpectedly encounter that cues the mind to enter an alternative state. Usually it is an environmental reminder that floods you with memories of a traumatic moment. A scent, sound, taste, sight, or texture can prompt a kind of time travel back to a previous state. Triggers make the body react as if you were back in the trauma. Your heart races, you feel nauseous. When my friend started talking about chemo, I was overcome with a helplessness and sadness that were larger than my capacity to stay present and connected. I had to leave the conversation.

I don't like that part of grief. I don't like that this has happened to me. I don't want to be so fragile. Or selfish. I want to be someone who listens well, someone who has the ability to be present for others. Before all the death, I was so skilled at getting out of my own way and showing up for emotionally tricky conversations. That is my vocation and was my superpower.

But it is different now.

Grief has left landmines in my psyche. I don't know when or how they'll get activated.

A friend posted photos of a family vacation in Montana.

In the airport, I hear a child's voice joyfully shriek, "Grandpa!"

I find my brother's snow boots in my garage.

My son finds a dead bird and insists that we must bury it and throw flowers in the lake.

I scroll through the D section in my phone contacts. And pass "Dad." And pass "Dave."

There are little spots scattered randomly inside of me that have the power to explode my homeostasis and push me into the abyss of grief.

I don't think I will linger here too long. I hope that time and healing will help me stay at the table and remain attentive and engage in the conversation. I hope that I will once again be able to listen and love others for their story without my story intruding.

But right now, it is too precarious. Never before has it felt so dangerous inside of me.

take a moment . . .

Usually triggers are sensory memories that our brains have encoded as a warning sign of danger or pain. They are sights, scents, sounds, tastes, or tactile memories that are directly or indirectly linked to painful experiences, and our brains pay special attention to those cues when it encounters them later.

When you think about the hardest moments of your loss, what sensory memories are relevant?

- What scenes, colors, images stand out in your memory?
- What scents were present (alcohol on someone's breath, the smell of baking bread when the phone rang)?
- What sounds do you remember (beeping hospital machines, breaking glass)?
- What tastes does your mouth recall (traces of blood, terrible gas station coffee)?
- What tactile sensations are relevant (the weight and scratchiness of a wool blanket, the coldness of someone's hands)?

Noting down the sensory components of your memories may help you have a better sense of your potential triggers. Write them down. Let them sit on the paper.

Perhaps thank your brain for keeping such careful track of these potential signs of pain. Thank your brain for working hard to help anticipate danger.

The reality is that triggers are painful, and none of us want to live with the looming threat of imploding. It is important to understand triggers and be compassionate toward what is happening in your mind. But you don't have to embrace them as a permanent fixture in your inner decor. Perhaps actively tell your brain that it doesn't have to work so very hard anymore—you are growing strong enough to remember without panic.

Here are a few simple strategies for coping with triggers:

- When you feel yourself beginning to respond to a trigger, give yourself alternative sensory input. Change your immediate situation by walking around the block, dabbing essential oil on the palm of your hand, turning on music, putting a piece of hard candy in your mouth, or splashing some water on your face. Give your sensory brain something significant to work with in the here and now so that it is not vulnerable to time travel without your consent.

- Create a mantra that grounds you to the present. Something as simple as "I'm here now." You could also try repeating the date or the name of where you are or describing your current context aloud to yourself. Orient to place, time, identity, and purpose, as I described in the first chapter.

- Another presence-grounding strategy is to pay very close attention to something in your immediate surroundings. Focus on the guacamole on the table. Count the chips in the bowl. Get your brain busy with the details of what is present right now.

Bottom line: be gentle.

You can order more guacamole tomorrow.

Pen in the Wash

A BALLPOINT PEN burst in the washing machine. Every single item of clothing had ink on it.

Death is like that.

It leaves a stain on everything in life.

Disney

Death and Murder for Children

I KNEW MY son was watching me. We were in the theater watching *Frozen 2* and inhaling fistfuls of popcorn. It was the scene in the latter half of the film where Anna believes that her sister, Elsa, is dead. Elsa is frozen solid at the bottom of a river, and Anna faces the realization that she must carry on life without her.

My son turns his body and looks directly at me, ignoring the film. He knows what's coming.

I begin to weep. This is what he expects. He pats my arm with his little hand, which is buttery from popcorn and sticky from sour gummy worms.

Anna's body slumps over, and her broken voice begins a haunting song of grief:

> *This grief has a gravity*
> *It pulls me down*[1]

Cartoon Anna and I together mourn our lost siblings. My young son comforts me while I cry.

As I think about it, it is such a twisted scene. Can't we just go to the movies, eat a bunch of crappy food, have a couple of laughs, and call it a night?

None of us intended for me to have a grief spiral from an animated film with a talking snowman and a plot line featuring a guy who is enmeshed with his fucking reindeer.

But the film is all about grief. It is about one daughter's quest to heal intergenerational trauma and right the wrongs of the past. It is about another daughter trying to learn the stories of her lost parents, and in so doing, she enters a space that is unsafe and threatens her life too.

I guess it is completely predictable that this story would remind me so much of my own family. My son certainly saw it coming. He's nine now. He knows that he has a mother who lives in grief. He knows that his mother has a wound where her brother once was and that the wound gets reopened from time to time. He's seen me cry more than I ever imagined he would.

Have you ever thought about how many children's films feature the death of a parent or sibling? Here are the ones that come to mind off the top of my head: *The Lion King*, *Frozen*, *Big Hero 6*, *The Land Before Time*, *Finding Nemo*, *How to Train Your Dragon 2*, *Bambi*, *Abominable*, *Vivo*, *Batman*, the entire *Star Wars* franchise. I'm sure there are more.

Death is so pervasive in children's films that a team of Canadian researchers looked at the prevalence of death in this genre and concluded that two-thirds of movies for kids depict the death of an important character while only half of films for adults did.[2] The researchers also found that the main characters in children's films were two and a half times more likely to die, and three times more likely to be murdered than the main characters in films marketed to adults.

So, if my kids watched a movie a week, they'd see thirty-four deaths a year—usually the death of a parent or close family member. What is up with that?

It is an easy plot device. What better way to thrust a character into a scenario in which they heroically redeem a terrible tragedy by going on a journey, taking back the throne, restoring the family name, and so on. The point of the movie becomes the main character rising again in the face of loss. It is the quintessential hero's journey.

I don't have issues with kids being exposed to death. I've had lots of open conversations about it with my kids. It is pretty normal for children to have some fear that the people they love will die. When children's films show children thriving after terrible events, there may be some psychological benefit to that. I suppose it could alleviate some fear by helping kids know that there is indeed life after death.

But I am worried about how the pervasiveness of these stories is shaping our expectations about grief. Children see death over and over, but there is very little treatment of grief. In most instances, the film shows the hero standing with head bowed beside an open grave. The audience may observe a tear or a nod toward a period of sadness, but the character is back in action within sixty seconds, fighting the dragon, building the robot, or saving the world.

The other alternative is that prolonged grief drives one to become a villain. If loss is not quickly translated into action, it seems to fester into vengeance and evil. I'm thinking of the Kingpin from *Spiderman*, Dr. Callaghan from *Big Hero 6*, Anakin Skywalker (a.k.a. Darth Vader) from *Star Wars*, Magneto from *X-Men*, among others. These characters were deeply wounded by grief, and it became the seed of evil.

These films are telling a story about grief that is a disservice to us all. Our society counts on a bereaved person bouncing back to action almost immediately. We expect the bereaved person to formulate a conquering plan that somehow sets right a terrible loss. And if they don't, in a prompt, timely manner, the suspicion is that the grief has ruined them. It isn't a helpful expectation. Or a fair timeline. These films help craft a society that has no model for the emotion of loss. For the slowness of it. For the darkness of it. Especially in the lives of children.

My children have been up close and personal with grief these past years. They've held human ashes in their hands. They anticipate that I will cry during a movie scene in which a character loses a sibling. They know all about cancer. They've attended memorials.

It isn't what I would have chosen for them—to be in a movie theater, comforting Mommy because the cartoon reminds her of her dead brother. That isn't what I ever pictured when I first held their tiny baby bodies in my arms and my heart swore to protect them with every cell in my body. Sometimes I apologize to them in whispers: "I'm sorry that our lives have unfolded like this."

My only hope is that they are learning about the reality of grief. They are seeing a more realistic picture than Disney will tell them. They're seeing me go to work, make pancakes, drive the car pool, laugh with my friends. They are seeing me live.

And they're seeing me cry.

They are also seeing that the duration of grief is not five minutes of screen time but that it is years.

When they came into my world, I didn't anticipate that grief would be such a prominent lesson in their childhood. But after watching Dave implode, alongside the loss of our dad, perhaps grief, real grief, is a more essential lesson that I anticipated. Perhaps watching me slog through it will help my children navigate out of their own darkness one day.

Disney is introducing them to death. It's my job to show them the reality of grief.

take a moment ...

Take a moment to remember your earliest impressions of death.

A character in a film or book? A grandparent? A beloved pet?

Perhaps you knew lots about death when you were a child.

How did your family of origin cope with death? Conversation? Ritual? Ceremonies? Scientific explanations? Silence? Did the grown-ups talk to you, or were you left to piece it together on your own? Did you see people cry, or were people expected to keep a stiff upper lip?

Were you scared, lost, confused? Did you feel guilty or angry?

How are your childhood experiences of loss relevant to you now?

In what ways is your approach to grief similar to that which was modeled by your family?

In what ways have you broken with those patterns?

It is important to assess the default settings that exist within you. Depending on age and life circumstance, many of us don't have a lot of opportunity to thoughtfully, intentionally choose our grieving strategies. Most of us are not taught how to grieve. We don't have a lot of practice with this set of emotions, so we operate from the implicit messages passed down by our families and/or our religious tradition. Grief is an emotional state that challenges our grown-up selves and often pulls us into a regression to early patterns. Our first experiences with grief stick with us. That is one reason it is so important to think through the context of your early history with death and grief. Perhaps the inherited approach to grief doesn't serve you right now.

Take a moment to write down and describe the approaches to grief to which you've been exposed. It is up to you to decide which logical explanations and emotional responses best serve you.

As you recall your early awareness of grief and death, picture your five-year-old or ten-year-old self (whatever age you were at the time of recognition).

With that child version of you at the forefront of your mind, shift your focus to the breath entering and exiting your body.

As you inhale, breathe in compassion and tenderness for your young self.

As you exhale, breathe out the childlike fear or confusion that still resides in your deepest recesses.

Don't Touch Anything

(and Bring Music)

FROM FEBRUARY 1, 2017, to May 10, 2019, I spent a lot of time in hospital rooms. Should you find yourself in such a situation, I've collected a few pro tips for you.

- Strategize your coffee. Coffee is freshest when the shifts change: 7:00 a.m., after lunch, 3:00 p.m., 8:00 p.m. Get coffee from the nurse's station, not from the waiting room. As long as it isn't behind the desk, this practice is permissible. This is especially true if it is the middle of the night. The waiting room coffee could be twelve hours old. I bring my own travel mug. It saves the environment, and I can control what it comes into contact with. I don't trust the stacks of paper or Styrofoam cups that are often in waiting rooms. It is too hard for people to touch just one cup. Therefore I'm terrified that all the cups have been touched by all the people. So, it is totally worth bringing your own cup or, worst case, forgoing the free coffee and trekking down to the cafeteria to procure coffee in a cup that has, hopefully, not been touched by many fingers.

- Actually, don't touch anything. This is an expansion of
  the recommendation about the waiting room coffee
  cups. Hospitals are petri dishes. I repeat, best not touch
  anything. I always kept a layer between my hand and
  any doorknob or elevator button. Even pre-COVID, I
  began to carry Lysol wipes in my backpack and hand
  sanitizer in my pockets. I am not a germ freak, but I
  heard some stories, enough stories to make me a germ
  freak in a hospital.

- Chum up with the medical staff. My dad was great
  at gabbing with the nurses. He learned their names.
  He swapped BBQ recipes and dog photos with them. He
  made friends. I'm pretty sure he got extra applesauce
  in the chemo room. And the friendly relationships
  seemed to make it a little bit more fun for him. It is
  easier to spend time in a hospital if you have some
  folks to banter with, people that you are happy to see
  despite the less than ideal reason for your meeting.
  As a frequent visitor to the hospital, I also found my
  relationships with the medical staff to be both helpful
  and enjoyable. On numerous occasions, they were able
  to organize specialist visits or treatment sessions so that
  I could be present. It was easier to navigate those things
  because I knew their names and the names of their dogs
  and whether they liked to ski or snowboard. I tried to
  make their lives easier with kindness and practical help
  whenever it was relevant. And in many small ways, I felt
  them trying to make my life easier.

- Make a good playlist. I reached out to friends, and they
  helped me create my "hospital sit" playlist on Spotify.
  Not too sad. Not too peppy. Emotionally nuanced
  but not emo. Mine featured Mumford & Sons, Ryan
  Adams, Fleet Foxes, Local Natives, the Mynabirds,

Trevor Hall, Cat Power, First Aid Kit, the Chainsmokers, the Wailin' Jennys, and some other random songs. Perhaps it doesn't sound like a big deal, but I assure you, you'll want a break from the beeping machines and the chatter in the hallway. You'll want a way to feel comfortable and at home in your own head when the environment lacks appeal. You'll want something to think about other than death or the quality of food in the cafeteria. I'm happy to share my hospital sit playlist if you find yourself in this situation. Having a playlist that you're into also helps you remember to bring your headphones, and as we've already discussed, headphones can be a helpful tool when you want to minimize interaction with the outside world.

• Grab a supply of junk magazines, poetry, and coloring books. I read *People* magazine in the hospital. I also read a lot of poetry, specifically Mary Oliver, Rupi Kaur, and Janne Robinson. Magazines are great because they are emotionally neutral. Poetry is great because it is emotionally rich and nourishing but contained in a small package. Magazines are for when the mind needs to disengage. Poetry is for when the heart needs to ground into an expression of words. And coloring books are helpful when the mind is restless and the heart is tired. Coloring books and music are a great combination in the late afternoon, when the day is wearing on and the beeping machines are causing a headache and you're out of energy to do or say or think about anything particularly meaningful.

• Wear layers. Hospitals always seem to be cold. But sometimes, in the afternoon, when the sun comes through the windows, the rooms can get really warm. I have a go-to sweater cape that can double as a blanket or pillow. It can be wrapped tightly around me if it is chilly or left open and flowing if I'm getting warm. It is important to be able to keep your body comfortable—because nothing else will be. The chairs are uncomfortable. Your heart and mind are uncomfortable. You might as well be physically comfortable with soft textures and good temperature regulation.

- Bring photos. Every time Dave had a long hospital stay, I filled his room with photos. Photos of him with his nephews, and with Rosy, our parents' dog. I brought photos of him in the mountains. I also brought photos when I went with my dad for his marathon chemo days. The photos served several purposes. First, they made the room homier, and less scary and artificial. Second, I wanted the photos to remind my brother and my dad of all the good parts of their lives. The places and the people they loved. I hoped the reminder would bring them a little energy or a little peace. Finally, and potentially most importantly, I wanted every member of the medical team to see that this was someone's brother, someone's son, someone's father. I wanted them to see beyond the chart and the body, beyond the words *addiction* or *cancer*. I wanted them to see that this is not a throwaway case of a suicidal drunk or terminally ill man who will certainly die soon. I wanted everyone to see that the individuals in those beds were people who were deeply loved. I hoped that would help them take a little bit more time and a little bit more care.

I hope that I am never again in a life situation that requires me to sit for days on end in a hospital. But the truth is, I will probably have to do it again. When it happens, I won't complain or drag my feet. Hospital sitting is an act of love. The only reason that I'll spend days and days in a hospital is because someone that I love is very sick. And if someone I love is very sick, you better believe that I will absolutely be there. Hospital sitting is love via presence. It is simple but deeply powerful, like the love from mommas and dadas who sit up, holding their sick babies through the night. There's nowhere else more important to be.

How to Survive
Memorial Services

Eat All the Cookies

WE HAD A memorial service for my dad.

He helped plan the shindig. He picked the songs for the video slideshow. He asked me to speak. He requested that his older sister, Kathy, colead the service. He requested that his grandsons play music. He did not want a viewing. He wanted to be cremated.

He had a hand in the whole thing.

Honestly, I'm sad that he wasn't able to attend. I think he would have had a nice time.

My favorite moment was when my youngest son came up to me during the after-service reception and sweetly said, "Momma, there are cookies here. Do you want a cookie?" In a moment of decadence, I said, "Oh, yes. Bring me one of every kind." I didn't know that it was a cookie buffet and that there were easily twenty plates of cookies laid out neatly on long church dining tables.

Dutifully, my dear child returned with a mischievous grin and presented me with a plate of cookies piled twenty high.

I accepted his challenge. For the remainder of the reception, I ate gobs of cookies from a mountainous pile while I chatted with my dead father's friends. I'm sure I spilled some. The plate was too full for me to notice and too unwieldy for me to stoop down to retrieve anything from the floor. It is possible that I left a trail of cookies marking my path like Hansel and Gretel's crumbs. I do feel a bit sorry for the church janitor who no doubt had to do some deep vacuuming that night.

People accept mildly crazy behavior from bereaved family members during memorial services.

When I was in junior high, I went to a memorial service for my flute teacher, Mrs. Fulkerth. She also died of cancer. She was young and had children my age and younger—they all had very interesting names that started with *J*. Mrs. Fulkerth had long dark hair that she wore in intricate braided buns, like a real-life Princess Leia. She was one of the most beautiful people I interacted with during my childhood. She was very kind and a great flute player. Her husband, Jeff, was devastated by her death. He walked into the memorial service several minutes late, wearing pink shorts and an old T-shirt. He seemed disoriented and looked disheveled. Everyone else was sitting politely, wearing church clothes. His out-of-place appearance made a significant impression on me, because church clothes were a big deal in my family. Shorts in church were an absolute no-no, and I couldn't quite understand why the man who seemed to love Mrs. Fulkerth so much couldn't manage to put on pants. I turned to my dad and asked him why Jeff was dressed *like that*. My dad was not a deeply tender person, but he had tears in his eyes when he said, "When someone's wife dies, they can wear whatever they want. No one worries about their clothes."

That was the first time I realized that grief necessitates the bending of some social rules. Or maybe it is more accurate to say that there is only one important rule for memorials: get through them.

I took that to heart with the cookies. When your dad dies, you can eat as many cookies as you want. My dad was no longer around to tell me not to. There were no glaring looks from across the room with the menacing dad face that says, "You're going to ruin your dinner."

I was unaware of anyone feeling concerned or phased by my giant tower of cookies. It would have made my dad laugh. And it made me laugh. And brought me a much-needed source of distraction. I had lots of conversations about my cookie pile that afternoon.

The worst part of the service was the pastor. He was a member of the staff at the church where we held the service, the church that my parents attended together for most of their adult lives. The pastor wasn't supposed to give a sermon; he was just supposed to welcome the community. My dad did not request a sermon, and not everyone in our family is a Christian, so a welcome from the pastor seemed like a nice nod to tradition without the ordeal feeling too churchy. I should also mention that my aunt is an ordained minister and that I am a seminary graduate with a master's degree in theology and significant preaching experience. We had it pretty well covered in terms of formal religious training.

I suppose the wishes of the dead do not fluster a man of God who's on a roll. The man went on and on about the notes that he found in my dad's old Bible. He tried to tell a story about my dad's legacy, the legacy of a man he hardly knew.

At one point he called him Tom. My dad's name was Tim.

That was the low point.

I was furious. I did my best to control my impulse to shift around in my seat, sigh loudly, or just blatantly roll my eyes. It was the part of the memorial service where I just had to hold my breath and get through.

Despite the pastor's mishap, I'm glad that we held a service for my dad. He wanted one. He lived his entire adult life in the same small city, and it felt right that we share his death and our grief with the many people he'd played racquetball with, met at the gym during the early morning hours, worked alongside, and sat next to in the pews. The ability to gather with others who'd known him over the years felt like an important part of the process. My childhood friends came. I recognized many of my father's friends, most of whom I hadn't seen since my wedding day.

I moved away from my hometown when I was seventeen, and I never went back to live there, just the occasional month or two between trips and jobs while I was in college. Having a funeral there, in that church, with that group of people, felt like an important return home. Even if it was a return home to say good-bye. It was an important ritual.

We did not have a formal memorial service for my brother.

It was too soon after Dad's death. We'd just done the rigma-role with out-of-town relatives, caterers, and printed obituaries. My mom was clear. She didn't want an event to grieve Dave. She wanted quiet and privacy.

About two months after Dave died, my remaining family came to visit Minnesota. That is when we planned a private memorial. My mom, my brother Dan, my husband and I, and our children doubled up on paddleboards and paddled out into Lake Bde Maka Ska on a bright July morning. It is the lake in Minneapolis very near my home and where Dave spent lots of time. When he didn't have work or treatment meetings, he'd ride his bike to my house, saunter into the kitchen, and ask if he could borrow a board. He'd hustle it across the street to the lake and spend the afternoon floating. For hours. He seemed to find tremendous peace there.

We retraced his path and paddled out to the center of the lake before eight on a Saturday morning. The July sun was bright, and the lake was perfectly still. We joined our paddle-boards into a single floating mass. We each released a fresh flower, a handful of Dave's ashes, and shared a memory or spoke a loving word about him. I don't remember what any-one else said. But I remember thinking that every word was perfect and that the children were deeply wise and that my mom was beautiful and brave. I couldn't get many words out. I think I said something simple like, "I miss you. Thank you for being so kind."

It was very precious to me. I'm glad that we did it that way.

We knew ourselves well enough to know that no number of cookies was going to get us through a formal event. Church clothes were too much. Frankly, clothes were too much. We wanted to honor him together, but the traditions weren't nurturing in this case, so we made a different plan.

There are no hard-and-fast rules about memorial services. I believe that some type of ritual or gathering is essential for grieving, but it certainly doesn't have to be the traditional church deal. The two services were very different. Both were perfect and both were flawed, but I'm very glad we listened to our hearts about what was helpful.

take a moment . . .

A memorial is something intended to remind or call up from memory. It also serves the purpose of solidifying or practicing memory.

Memory is somewhat subjective. There's very little absolute, objective truth in our recall of people or events, especially those that hold a lot of emotion for us. Intentionally or not, we choose which elements of memory we "practice." Memorial services function as a corporate repository of memory. Stories are exchanged. Photos are shared. They are occasions of collective remembering.

The shared memory and communal aspect of memorial services are super important for the grieving process. However, these events are doomed to be somewhat painful and awkward, because grief is so personal and a gathering of grieving people is always going to be a gathering of people who are out of sync with one another. No two people are grieving in the same way. No two people had the same relationship with the one that was lost. Yet in a collective gathering, there is pressure to conform to a unified story, a set of shared feelings and experiences. Memorial services touch on big conversations about religion, money, old family wounds, and emotional expression. They are ripe for touchy moments and meltdowns.

It is a 100 percent guarantee that some part of a memorial gathering will feel off to you.

That doesn't mean don't do one. They *are* important. But it does mean that it is best to attend with your coping resources primed and ready to go.

Strategies for formal memorial services:

- Protect your energy. Anticipate that it will be hard. Don't hesitate to make the day what you need it to be. Take time to go for a run, take a few minutes for yoga, or have a quiet cup of coffee or a nourishing meal of your choosing. Try to fuel your body and your inner self with what is most helpful. There will be lots of people around, but it is perfectly okay to take some quiet time for yourself.

- Gather your team. Ask for practical help with basics like food, child wrangling, and transportation. I asked a few friends to sit behind my family and intervene if my kids got squirrely. I asked my husband to linger nearby during the reception, and we created a hand signal that I could use if I wanted him to save me from an overwhelming conversation.

- Honor your preferences. Give yourself the space to eat what you want, wear what you want, leave when you want, and talk to whom you want. This event is happening because some dark force, outside of your control, crept in and disrupted your life and the lives of those you love. You did not have a choice about the events that caused the memorial in the first place. You've likely not had much control over the organization of the memorial service. You're drowning in events not of your choosing. It is okay to choose some details for yourself.

If a formal service is not the best option for you, or if you attend one but it is not meaningful for you, create a personalized memorial.

Take time to collect special photos and physical reminders of the
one that you lost. Place them in a special box along with a blank
journal or set them neatly on a table. Set a reminder in your calendar
to write a memory in the journal every few days, once a week—
the pace is up to you. Create your own time and place in which
to practice memory. Because it is helpful to memorialize with
others, consider inviting close friends or family members for a
night of remembrance on your terms. Look at photos, tell stories,
cook a favorite meal, listen to the lost one's favorite music. Be
together in memory.

The Emotional Power
of Office Supplies

OF ALL THE things that my father acquired over the course of his life, these are the possessions I kept:

- His high school ring. It is gold with a big T (for Tim).
  It is not valuable—maybe worth a few hundred
  dollars. And I never saw him wear it, so it doesn't
  have a lot of memory attached to it. The ring always
  resided in the wooden jewelry box on his dresser, the
  one that I would illicitly explore as a child. It was
  full of cuff links, some rings and other jewelry, and
  odds and ends, a stray key. This ring fits on my ring
  finger, which makes me laugh. Were his fingers that
  slender when he was a young man? How did he ever
  wear it? On his pinky? On a chain around his neck?
  Perhaps he ordered the wrong size, which accounts
  for why the ring seemed to live its entire life in the
  wooden box.

  Now it sits on my dresser in a little container
  with my other rings. When I remember, I wear
  it on the tenth of the month. I also wear it in
  May, which is his birthday month.

- Puma sweatpants. Dark blue, size small. These are the most comfortable sweatpants ever. He bought them long after cancer ravaged his body and moved him from size large to size small. My pre-cancer dad could never wear size small. The irony is that these are my most favorite of my inherited possessions. In the winter, they are part morning uniform. If I'm not going immediately to the gym, I pull them on to get warm and cozy before walking downstairs to start the fire and the coffee. Or if it is a cold day, and I don't have anything professional to do, I might wear them all day. I wear them at some point in the day, four to five days a week. And they always remind me of my dad. I can see him in his recliner, TV remote in hand, watching the 49ers play. These twenty-five-dollar sweatpants are the object of deepest comfort and connection.

- Flannel shirts. The week of my dad's death, I rifled through his closet and found some soft flannel shirts—size: Men's XL. They were from his pre-cancer body. One is blue plaid, the other is red plaid. I slept in them like an old-fashioned nightgown the week that I stayed in my parents' home, keeping vigil while he died. I took them home with me. I sometimes wear the blue one with leggings and a belt and boots. It's a look one can only pull off in Minnesota. I call it snow-glam.

  The other shirt—the red one—I gave to Dave when he was in the hospital so that he didn't have to wear those cold cotton gowns. He was so grateful to receive it. A little hug from dad.

  I don't know what happened to it after he died. It is probably on the rack at the Salvation Army thrift store somewhere in Montana.

- Office supplies. My dad was type A. His desk was
  very well organized. He would know—and growl—if
  a pen was moved from its place. Moving something
  on his desk was one of the top five things that I
  got yelled at for as a kid. Which tells you both how
  well-behaved I was and how important his office
  supplies were to him. Upon his death, I found bags of
  highlighters sorted by color, bags of Sharpies sorted
  by tip width, and bags of nice Easy-Glide writing
  pens sorted by color (blue and black). I took them
  all. I also removed from his desk the following items:
  three stacks of Post-it notes, four wrapped packages
  of unopened index cards, one pair of Apple earbuds
  (the old kind with the cord), one Maglite, and one
  Swiss Army knife.

That's pretty much it. That's all I inherited. Or rather, that's all I wanted to inherit. My dad didn't accumulate a lot of material wealth during his life, and I'm not very sentimental about things. My mom gave my brothers and me free rein to take what we wanted—but all I wanted were these few simple things.

She later sent my kids all my dad's flashlights, camp lights, headlamps—which was a great gift for them.

It seems like she spent the year after his death trying to sort through and give away most of his things. It was a big project. One of the many administrative tasks that goes along with death that you're not really aware of until you get there. He had sixty-five years' worth of stuff.

In stark contrast, by the time my brother died, he had almost nothing. I found a pair of his snow boots in my garage. Most of his clothing and personal items were lost before he moved back to Montana when his apartment manager had to hire a biohazard team to clean his apartment after the suicide attempt. It seems they just took everything, including his guitar and his books and journals. That never seemed right to me.

When he died, he had only a bike, a small suitcase, and a back-pack. The sheriff sent most of that to my mom. The bike and clothes were donated.

We spend so much of our lives acquiring and managing possessions and, in the end, very little of it matters. My dad took meticulous care of his car. We sold it the day after he died because my mom needed the cash. We had no attachment to it, even though it was important to him.

The things that I love are the things that intimately remind me of my dad—his clothing, reflections of his eccentricities, or items that held sentimental significance to him.

In the end the stuff doesn't matter, but my memory of his love matters so deeply.

take a moment . . .

What are your favorite objects? Things given to you by your loved one? Things they left behind that you've picked up and made part of your day-to-day?

Is there an object of clothing that reminds you of a hug? Something that brings to mind very mundane but important parts of how they spent their moments? A coffee cup. A favorite pen. It is okay to integrate these items into your day-to-day. Not all memorials have to be regarded as sacred. Not all heirlooms require lock and key. Let your memorials reflect the life you shared together.

Sweatpants and highlighters can become a shrine.

Busy Hands and Open Hearts

AFTER MY SECOND year of graduate school, I spent a summer studying Spanish and backpacking through Central America. During my weeks in El Salvador, I found a temporary home in the guestroom of a woman named Ana Maria. Ana Maria ran an informal boardinghouse and a small *pupuseria* from her home, which was located a few blocks from the University of El Salvador (in San Salvador). She was a middle-aged rotund woman who had become the surrogate mother of the neighborhood. She was generally soft-spoken but was not shy about scolding her regulars for running late to class. She advised boyfriends and girlfriends on relationship matters, lectured young women who were wearing tummy-revealing tank tops, talked politics with professors, and counseled young mothers on the care of their children, all while chopping cabbage and frying *pupusas*.

One morning, over a quiet breakfast, she told me her story. During El Salvador's civil war (1979–1992), her neighborhood was a hotbed of conflict. Student protesters clashed with government forces, informants monitored left-leaning faculty and other members of the intelligentsia. On a Tuesday afternoon Ana Maria's sixteen-year-old son was taken while walking down the street in broad daylight.

He had come home for lunch, returned to school, and never came back. He *was disappeared* (the passive verb when translated directly from the Spanish is worth preserving). *He* didn't disappear, *someone else* disappeared him. It is possible that he was killed right away. It is possible that he was forced to fight, then killed later. It is unlikely, but possible, that he is alive somewhere. She does not know. She will likely never know.

Two months after her son's disappearance, her husband died of a heart attack. He died from a broken heart.

Ana Maria told me that every time her door opens, she looks to see if it is her son returning. Every time, she feels a twinge of disappointment that it is not him.

After she lost her son and her husband, she spent two years closed away in her home. She prayed for death. She fell into the depths of depression with no energy to fight back.

One day a teenage boy knocked on her door and asked if she had any extra food. That was a common occurrence in a time of war and poverty, but this time something clicked in her. She wanted to help. She wanted to feed him. She invited him in and cooked him a meal.

The next day he returned and brought some others. They brought some corn and left a few coins on the table. The next day again. The next day again.

For the past ten years Ana Maria has been cooking pupusas for students and university folks and various neighbors. Her enclosed porch is filled with plastic tables and chairs. She begins cooking at 10:00 a.m. and doesn't finish until midnight every day of the week. University students, professors, miscellaneous travelers, and lost souls find a meal and a momentary home at Ana Maria's. Her son's former bedroom has become a cozy room for rent for travelers like me.

Her pain is close to the surface. She tells her story openly. My tears join hers as we sit together in her kitchen drinking morning coffee. We pass a tissue box back and forth.

She continues to cry almost daily. She continues to grieve often and openly. She has not stopped longing for her son and her husband, but she has continued to live.

In many moments during my weeks with her, I witnessed Ana Maria move seamlessly between grief and joy. She teased and chided, lectured, and counseled. She presided over the kingdom of her porch with a matriarchal fortitude that is both loving and not at all to be messed with. Her life embodies the coexistence of grief and love.

I watched her closely. I couldn't know at that time that I was preparing myself for my own grief, that I was watching and learning the elegant dance between deep sadness and deep joy. I could not know she was teaching me how to love in an openhearted way. Before staying with her, I may have been under the assumption that her level of loss would shatter a person in a way that would leave them permanently depressed, numb, or locked in a dance of escape. I might have cracked open my diagnostic books to find a suitable diagnosis for someone experiencing prolonged bereavement or chronic depression. After all, she was crying every day. But no. The only thing "wrong" with Ana Maria was her deep sense of love. She didn't try to escape, numb, or intellectualize. She didn't cut off her pain or restrict her capacity for the full range of experience. She let it all coexist inside of her.

She kept her hands busy. She made her moments useful. She forced herself to get up every morning. She surrounded herself with young people, thinking people, hungry people, appreciative people. She told her story. She listened to the stories of others.

She taught me that humans are stronger than I thought. Pain hurts. It changes us. It becomes part of us.

She showed me how to grieve without breaking. And I had no idea how much I would need to know about that.

take a moment . . .

Who are your grief heroes?

Who are the people in your world who have walked through significant pain and seem to have come out on the other side? Beyond Ana Maria, some that come to my mind are Viktor Frankl, Joan Didion, Nelson Mandela, a woman that I used to go to church with named Linda-Jean.

Pick one or two grief heroes and order a book about them (if they're well known) or schedule a phone call with them (if you know them).

Write down who they are and why you admire them.

Explore what they might have to teach you in this phase of your life. How did they navigate their grief?

These grief heroes do not exist to shame you with thoughts of *It could have been so much worse*. They are brought to mind to remind you that you are not alone in your struggle and that many people, people like you, have found their way through to the other side of darkness.

Your experience is unique.

But you are not the first human who is trying to learn how to come back to life.

PART TWO

cancer

This Is Not What I Ordered

MY DAD WENT to the doctor because he had a lingering flu.

A month before the visit to the doctor, our family had been together for Christmas, near Santa Cruz, California. He'd played baseball on the beach with his grandsons and organized our Christmas feast. He and I went out alone early one morning to let Rosy the golden retriever run at the dog beach. There were many perfect moments on that trip.

After returning from Christmas, he felt off. He was tired and sluggish, like he was fighting a cold. He suspected that his precious grandchildren had shared a bug that his body was busily fighting off. After a few weeks of rest and hydration (my family's remedy for anything from a toothache to a broken heart), he finally went to his doctor.

In a quick twist of the afternoon plan, his doctor sent him directly to the hospital. His blood count was very low, and he was severely anemic. His doctor feared that something was very wrong, something much worse than the flu.

That was the beginning of the crazy.

My dad left the hospital several days later, after a blood transfusion and a diagnosis of esophageal cancer.

And just like that, life would never be the same.

By the time the tumor was discovered, it was a ten-centimeter monster along the length of his esophagus, and it had grown all the way through the esophageal wall. As far as tumors go, it was giant.

Cancer is so sneaky. The tumor had been growing and growing. Silently. For years. Taking over his body undetected, uninvited.

While he was watching football, it was growing.

While he was making scrambled eggs, it was growing.

While he was sleeping, it was growing.

While he was clipping his toenails, it was growing.

According to the Mayo Clinic website, these are the risk factors for esophageal cancer:

1 Having gastroesophageal reflux disease
2 Smoking
3 Having Barrett's esophagus
4 Being obese
5 Drinking alcohol
6 Having bile reflux
7 Having an abnormal esophageal sphincter
8 Having a steady habit of drinking very hot liquids
9 Not eating enough fruits and vegetables
10 Undergoing radiation treatment to
   the chest or upper abdomen[1]

Of these risk factors, my father had exactly one: reflux. He popped a lot of TUMS.

Never in his life did my dad drink alcohol or smoke. He exercised religiously every day. He didn't even drink coffee, so no worry about the dangerous hot beverages noted in number 8. He ate his fruits and veggies.

As a coffee drinker and bourbon aficionado, I have more risk factors for esophageal cancer than he did.

It really was unexpected.

A heart problem, yes, that would have been expected. He was type A: anxious, rushed, and high strung. He'd had a heart attack and triple bypass when he was forty-nine. A heart problem would have made sense.

A joint problem, yes, that would have been expected. He'd already had many surgeries on his knees, hips, ankles, and shoulders. His joints were a mess of old sports injuries and osteoarthritis. In high school, I did a biology project about his high tibial osteotomy, a surgery that he'd had to remove a section of his hip bone and place it into his lower leg to alleviate the pressure caused by uneven wearing of the cartilage in his knees. He was a bionic man.

That's how it is with this kind of cancer. It is rarely detected until it is massive enough to make it hard to eat or swallow. And by then it is usually too late to do very much about it.

My dad was private and tenacious. Without knowing it, I expected him to march on into his eighties, becoming increasingly grumpy and reclusive, with the television elevated to higher and higher decibels. I expected him to care for my mom as her multiple sclerosis advanced. I expected him to outlast her. And then I expected him to slip silently into death one night in his sleep, his heart eventually failing without pomp or circumstance.

I can appreciate how these words sound. It is idyllic and perhaps entitled or maybe childlike to respond to cancer with, "This is not what I expected." I sound like I'm at a restaurant trying to explain to the waiter, "No, I didn't order the Cobb salad. I ordered the Caesar salad. Please bring me the Caesar salad." This is not what I ordered. This was not even on my mental menu.

This is not what I expected.

More than anything, that phrase reflects confusion.

I spent a few years teaching statistics to psychology undergrads. I'd get so excited trying to rally them to the cause and enthuse them into greater statistics affection. Most psychology students don't show up with a love for math. I would try to convince them that statistics are a powerful tool to help predict and solve important and interesting human problems: We can use statistical tools to identify risk factors, and then we can use statistical tools to identify how to prevent those problems strategically before they occur. Statistical probability is the closest thing we have to a crystal ball, or a time machine. Or magic. If we do the math right, we can (kind of) foresee the future before it happens.

My college students didn't find me that compelling. I may have oversold it. Or maybe they just resented my energy at eight in the morning.

When it came to esophageal cancer and my dad, there were not very many risk factors, and there were lots of protective factors, so statistically speaking, his getting esophageal cancer was an unlikely event.

My scientist friends are gently saying, "Sherry, that is not how statistics work. Statistics are based on group predictability and on large numbers. Risk and protective factors don't reliably predict individual outcomes."

I know. It just isn't what I expected.

The phone call came the day after my family and I had returned home from a week's vacation in Mexico. We'd been at a beautiful resort, escaping the Minneapolis winter. Our trip was lovely and carefree. I made everyone get up to watch a sunrise. My kids ordered sugary drinks from a swim-up bar. Little did we know that it would be our last worry-free vacation for years to come.

My dad called to tell me that he was going to the hospital. That he was anemic. They were going to do some tests. His voice sounded worried. It sounded young. I could hear the fearful child within the voice of the full-grown man.

It was not what he expected either.

take a moment . . .

Give yourself the space to notice all the things that have surprised or shocked you about the entrance of grief into your life. Note down the moments or events that "shouldn't" have happened according to the foundational narrative in your head: the curveballs, the occurrences that no one would have predicted, and moments where you had the breath knocked out of you.

These specific moments may not represent the most traumatizing or saddest part of your loss; they may not be the *worst* moments. However, absorbing a shock is a distinct human experience. Unexpected news pulses through us like electricity and can leave us feeling burned and frayed inside.

Notice the shock-absorbing instants in your story. Write them down so that you can begin to soothe and heal those injured, fried cells. The goal is to replace shock with self-compassion, and helpless fear with tenderness.

Here's an example: I close my eyes and recall the moment of receiving that phone call from my dad. I notice the internal clenching and elevated heart rate that goes with that memory. I put my hands on my chest to feel my heart and my breath. I pay attention to the pressure and warmth of my hands pressing to my center. I intentionally slow my breath. I ask my heart to slow down. I imagine filling my heart space with warmth, with a kind of glowing warm flame that heats the inner room of my chest. It is comfortable and nourishing. I can relax in it. I linger in this new inner space as I picture the phone in my hand and my dad's voice in my ear.

With my mind, I affirm that my heart is big enough to hold this news.

The memory of the shocked, breathless, pale woman on the phone becomes the image of a woman whose heart is warm and alive with tender strength. I shift into compassion for my dad and for myself.

You've had to absorb a shock and pivot your life, probably in an instant. Give yourself credit for how hard that is. In your active imagination, grant yourself retroactive grace.

Fight or Surrender?

MY DAD WAS a fighter. A lifelong athlete. A determined, get-up-early, bounce-back, beat-the-odds kind of guy.

When he received a cancer diagnosis, he seemed to quickly toss aside his unmet expectations and go into cancer-fighting mode. Full-on battle stance. Chemo, radiation, clinical trials, immunotherapy, major diet modification, regimented exercise—anything and everything was on the table for him. He drove across the country for an evaluation at the Mayo Clinic, one of the best hospitals in the world. They have a whole team of experts who focus on the assessment and treatment of esophageal cancer. He took the medications and followed the plan of attack.

"I'm going to beat this," he'd say. "There's more to try. I've got more fight in me."

I sent him a bright purple T-shirt that said "Lean, Mean, Cancer-Fighting Machine."

We were a sports family. Depending on the season, the television channel was tuned to whatever favorite team was playing on a given night. San Francisco 49rs, San Francisco Giants, Los Angeles Lakers, Indiana University basketball, Notre Dame football, the Indy 500, the Olympics—sports were the backdrop of our family life.

When there weren't evening games to watch, my family gathered in the living room for sports-oriented movies. Our favorite films were about people who beat the odds and came out on top, those who didn't quit, those who pushed through to the end and the eventual victory. *Hoosiers* and *Rudy* were required annual viewing. (Did I mention that my parents grew up in Indiana?)

My brothers and I all played baseball, just as my dad had throughout his childhood and young adult years. My dad would host outside batting practice and fielding drills for us every evening in the spring, beginning as soon as we could walk.

For fighters, the basic assumption is that the right amount of effort, coaching, and self-discipline will prevail. The athlete will endure. The hero will win.

This was such a deep part of our family culture because my mom was diagnosed with multiple sclerosis a year after I was born. The fighting philosophy cemented itself right then and there: *Never quit. Keep going. One step at a time.* This served us well in many ways. There was no room for victim mentality in our family. Despite her illness, my mom was a tireless parent, a hard worker, and a source of support to many. It never occurred to her to complain or mope or see herself or her life as limited. She's tenacious, resilient, and as tough as they come. And she has lived a very full, active life despite forty years with MS.

All this strength and stick-to-itiveness is mostly a gift. But the truth is, there are some downsides, and the limitation of a fighting spirit became clearer to me the further we went into the cancer journey. The universal secret is that every fighter will lose. Somehow. Somewhere. To something.

Stage IV metastatic esophageal cancer is a dragon of an opponent. A tumor the length and width of the esophageal wall. Tumors in the lymph nodes. Tumors in the lungs. Tumors in the liver. Eventually, tumors in the brain.

It was never a winnable fight. I looked up the prognosis projections the day he received his diagnosis—me and statistics. The two-year survival rate for stage IV metastatic cancer was less than 10 percent. The five-year survival rate was less than 3 percent. It was highly unlikely that he would defeat this disease.

No one likes that story.

I sat with him a few weeks after the initial diagnosis, when the Mayo Clinic team explained the diagnosis and the staging.

The Mayo doctor told my dad and my mom and me that the cancer was officially stage IV. He used the word *metastatic*, which everyone knows is universally bad. He used the term *very advanced*.

For me, the room began to spin.

But my dad jumped straight into fight mode without missing a beat.

> First question: "When do you want to do surgery
>   to remove this thing?"
> Mayo doc's response: "We cannot remove this tumor,
>   Tim. Your treatment plan does not include surgery."
> Second question: "Okay. So, are you going to use
>   radiation to zap it out?"
> Mayo doc's response: "We cannot use radiation on
>   your esophagus, Tim. Your treatment plan does
>   not include radiation."
> Third question: "Well, chemo . . . I don't really want
>   to lose my hair, but I'll do it."
> Mayo doc's response: "Yes, Tim. We have some
>   good chemotherapy options to help shrink the
>   tumor and prevent future growth."
> Fourth question: How long do you think I'll need to
>   be on chemo?
> Mayo doc's response: "You will be on chemo for the
>   rest of your life."

The rest of your life.

That one took my breath away. Those words solidified it for me. There was no coming back from this. The terms *remission*, *cure*, and *cancer-free* were never part of the conversation. The cancer was going to be with my dad to the end. It was going to be the end.

I don't think my dad could fully absorb it. When the doctor said "The rest of your life," my dad seemed to shake his head slightly—the same motion that boxers make after they've taken a punch and been knocked down but have the footing to pop right back up. They're on their feet, but are dazed. As a fighter, my dad fundamentally believed in his own ability to beat the odds with the right combination of effort, discipline, and medical expertise.

All told, my tenacious fighting father did thirty-six rounds of chemotherapy in eighteen months. Some at the Mayo Clinic, some at the local hospital in Redding, and some at UC Davis, where he eventually participated in a clinical trial for an experimental medication. He tried at least five different combinations, modified dosages, and eventually anything experimental that the doctors would throw his way.

None of it really made a dent.

About nine months after his diagnosis, he called me one day, and his voice sounded so strange—an odd mix of discouraged and amused. "I lost my eyelashes," he said. Neither of us was sure whether to laugh or cry. He handled lots of terrible moments like a champion. But the eyelashes seemed like one step too far.

I hopped onto Amazon and sent him a box of garish, fake eyelashes. They were the kind that can be adhered to eyelids with tiny sticky tape and were adorned with glitter and rhinestones. It was the only way I knew to respond to the mounting tiny injuries that were beginning to threaten to undo him.

Six months before he died, he began to fall. The tumor had spread to his brain and taken space near his brain stem, which dysregulated his balance and made him constantly dizzy. My mom came into the house after taking the dog outside to find him unconscious on the kitchen floor.

I was in Nicaragua when this happened. I was there with my eldest son, visiting dear friends, playing in the ocean, hiking volcanoes. My dad left me a message that I have never deleted from my phone. His voice was so different. Sad and scared. Lost.

I spoke to the doctor. It was bad. There were two separate tumors in the brain, one near the base of the brain stem and one in the frontal lobe. My dad wanted to do radiation to try to shrink the tumor. I gently tried to discourage him from more treatment, but he wanted to move forward.

We didn't talk on the phone very much after that. I think he found it difficult to know what to say. There were no play-by-play accounts of cancer-fighting battles to regale me with. It was the same update: "I am getting sicker and sicker. My head hurts. I'm dizzy. I am dying." But he never wanted to say that to me. So he didn't talk much.

Looking back, I wish that he hadn't fought so hard.

I wish he'd heard the diagnosis for the death sentence that it was and acted accordingly.

What would you do if you knew that you had eighteen months to live?

You wouldn't spend it in hospital waiting rooms or sitting in front of crappy daytime TV while you're hooked up to IV pumps.

I wish he'd skipped those appointments with well-meaning physicians and gone to sit by the beach or spent afternoons in a canoe with his grandkids. Or talked to me about how he felt. About his life. About my life. About what it was like to be moving on from this life. I wish he'd shared some poignant end-of-life wisdom so that my brothers and I could end our father's story with a sense of fullness and completion.

But all his energy went into fighting. I offered to take him and our entire family on a cruise to Alaska. He'd never been, and it was on his bucket list. I had the money and I had the time. However, he declined my offer because he was uncomfortable missing any chemo appointments. We didn't have that one last adventure together.

I wish more of his energy had gone into dying well, into living the last eighteen months of his life with as much ease and connection as possible. Maybe he would have had less time, but perhaps more time of his choosing. Perhaps better time.

From where I sit, the fight to win kept my dad from surrendering to the struggle and coming up for air long enough to see his wife, his children, and his grandchildren in their fear and sadness. It kept him from us.

He fought so that he could stay, but the irony is that the fight meant we lost parts of him earlier than we had to.

It was not my decision to make. While he was alive, I never expressed anything but support for his desire to throw as much medical force against his cancer as he could. I cheered him on and offered only an occasional gentle comment like, "I wonder if another clinical trial is worth it." I let him know my perspective, but I never criticized his choice.

It was his choice.

My friend Kelsey was diagnosed with cancer, and she had a 17 percent survival prognosis. She fought and she won. And she's still here, hanging out with her kids and texting me photos of the totem poles she encounters on RV trips. I suppose that could have been my dad. He could have been one of the three out of one hundred people who survive longer than five years with stage IV esophageal cancer.

I might make exactly the same decision if I end up in his shoes. I don't know what it feels like to have a monster cancer lingering in my body. I might find that I'm equally eager to cut it out, burn it out, poison it, or utilize whatever aggressive means are available to me to try to rid myself of the monster.

Fighting gave him something to do, a reason to get up in the morning. It helped him overlook the misery of cancer and believe that he may have some agency or some power over what was threatening him.

My dad was not a quitter. He was stubborn, tenacious, easily frustrated, and a downright pain in the ass to be in an argument with.

He approached cancer in the same way he approached his life. And as was true of many aspects of our relationship, I didn't agree with him, but I did respect him.

take a moment . . .

Major losses tap into our deepest, oldest, most primal scripts. My dad's decision to fight, armed with every possible medical resource, was consistent with his worldview and understanding of how one copes with threat.

The decisions about medical intervention and life-threatening illnesses are complex and highly personal.

One of the challenges of grief is that there's nothing left to fight. There are no medical treatments or cancer-killing diets to try. There are no more specialist appointments or books to read. The fight is over, and death has mandated surrender.

The fighters of the world have a hard time with grief. The drive to fight can keep us from being present to grief, from doing the work of grief.

There's wisdom in fighting, and there's wisdom in surrender.

I suppose the deepest wisdom is in knowing which phase you're in.

I feel like a former fighter. Like someone who's hung up her boxing gloves and is now nursing the chronic aches and pains that are the residue of all those bouts. My conscious shift from fight to surrender has been important to my grief. It is the shift toward acceptance, toward stillness, toward nothingness. I'm finding relief in the quiet of it.

Perhaps consider where you are in the continuum of fight to surrender.

Is there some enemy left to fight? Do you feel tense, active, powerful energy stirring inside of you? Is your mind busy with potential strategies, defenses, and alternatives?

Is this fight-energy serving you right now? Or is it a leftover strategy from an earlier time?

How does it feel to entertain the possibility of surrender? Can you settle into it? Can you wave the proverbial white flag and allow your tiredness to ease you into rest? Surrender is the beginning of the journey toward finding peace with all that you could not will into being. It is the beginning of comfort for your battle-scarred heart.

Here's the mantra: *There's nothing left to do. What has happened, has happened. I'm here now.*

Don't surrender too soon. But don't fight too long. Trust your instincts about when it is time to let go.

Middle-Class Cancer

IF YOU'RE GOING to get really sick in America, try to make sure you have a lot of money or almost no money. Don't be in the middle.

Money was a complicated issue in our cancer story.

Ironically, when my dad came from California to Minnesota's Mayo Clinic, money was not an issue. As one of the preeminent hospitals in the world, they had pretty much figured out the money thing. They billed Medicare and had grants to cover the rest. My dad didn't pay a cent for some of the best medical care in the world.

But when it came time to return home, Medicare didn't cover everything. There was a hefty share of cost, and he began receiving medical bills for thousands of dollars.

My parents had $15,000 in their savings account. It was their entire savings. They didn't own a home; they owned two simple cars.

Their savings was too much money to qualify them for a low-cost insurance supplement that would cover the thousands of dollars that Medicare didn't cover. Not to mention that it is a bit tricky to get an insurance supplement when you have terminal cancer. Cancer is expensive.

Basically, they had the choice of spending their savings to fight the cancer, thereby leaving my mom with fewer assets if my dad did die, or forgo treatment because it was cost prohibitive.

They even discussed the possibility of getting a "medical divorce." A divorce that would legally separate their assets so that my mom could keep their savings and my dad would be poor enough for full health coverage. It would also protect my mom from having to pay any outstanding costs after my dad died.

Although legally convenient, my mom wouldn't hear of it. They had been married for forty-five years. She wasn't going to get a divorce over some simple math.

What a crazy choice.

As a work-around, my parents gifted me $10,000, which sat in my savings account.

That made them officially poor enough for supplemental Medi-Cal insurance to cover the Medicare share of cost. And it was below the IRS gift limit, so we could slide through without incurring IRS scrutiny. I'm not sure if our plan was completely legal, but if anyone would like to prosecute me, I would welcome the chance to fight about it in court.

Although I'm guessing "the system is stupid" is perhaps not the best legal argument.

I never touched the money, of course. It was their money.

For the remaining year of his life, my proud, hardworking, self-sufficient father had to text me every time he needed some cash transferred back into his bank account.

I hated that.

As if the cancer wasn't taking enough away from him already, he deserved the dignity of keeping his own money in his own bank account.

And still be able to afford treatment he desired.

take a moment...

It is helpful to list the small indignities. The little things that hurt. The death-by-a-thousand-paper-cuts kind of things. The roll-my-eyes, you've-got-to-be-kidding-me kind of things.

I don't suggest that you list these things to whine or "sweat the small stuff."

I suggest noticing the small hurts because it is easy to disregard them and, eventually, they add up to become a very big pile of pain. Losing eyelashes. Losing the freedom to keep your money in your own bank account. These are tiny parts of the larger story of dying—but they make the loss much harder.

The little indignities need their own journal page. The little losses warrant their little griefs. The microaggressions to your soul.

Name them. Feel them. Release them.

Once again, give yourself credit for all the shit you've had to wade through.

Touching Two Worlds

TWO WEEKS BEFORE my dad died, I was in Paris, having dessert two blocks from the Eiffel Tower. My family and I had a long layover on the way home from a magical vacation in Croatia. We were all bright and shiny from beaches and waterfalls and exploring ancient cities. I'd promised our daughter that I'd take her to Paris. And to Paris we went. For twenty-four hours we loaded up on fancy desserts, cheese, and a whirlwind tour of the City of Lights.

We arrived home happy and tired and set about the task of decorating our house for Halloween. Despite the tight timeline, we threw together fantastic costumes and spent October 31 trick-or-treating until the kids were laden with candy and begging to go to bed.

On November 2, I flew home to Redding, the town in which I was born and raised.

On November 10, my dad died.

In the last week of his life, he shifted from one who was fighting to one who was dying. In my mind, I've labeled the last week "The Dying Week." For those eight days I went home to help with dying.

The day after I arrived home, I sat next to him in the cancer center while he received fluids. It was his last day of treatment before surrendering the fight and entering hospice care.

While I sat beside him, I worked on a book proposal, responded to emails from consulting clients, and talked with colleagues about partnership opportunities. I sat there, living in the world of the future, making the plans of the healthy and the strong. I also sat there knowing I was with one who was dying. And dying soon.

It was (and is) so much to hold: the expanse of a beautiful world that is waiting to be explored. The sweet, noisy delight of my wild young ones collecting candy on a cold October night. The energy inside me that sparks me to write, to speak, to reach out, to create. The beauty and energy of a world-class city just waiting to be explored.

And then there is the quiet, cold sadness of loving someone who is dying. The consuming focus on breath and movement and fluid and pain. The inevitable reality of a body that is growing smaller and colder and weaker by the minute. The tears that flow intermittently throughout the day.

I'm part of what social scientists call the sandwich generation, one of those in middle adulthood who is both caring for children and caring for aging and ill parents. It is the most responsible "adulting" phase of life, one in which I am sandwiched between the work of helping people whom I love to begin their lives and also helping people whom I love to complete theirs.

It feels like emotional whiplash. To move back and forth between joy and grief, between those who are beginning and those who are ending. Between what is being built and what is falling apart. Between my own aliveness and the deep reality of the death that will come to him, to me, to all of us.

It would be easier if I ignored or numbed or intellectualized or in some way protected myself from *feeling* the whole range of it.

But ease and comfort have never been my ambition. So I steadied my breath and jumped headlong into the business of expanding. Of becoming wide enough to reach to the edge of joy with one set of fingertips and the edge of grief with the other set.

To be present to all of it.

take a moment . . .

Let's practice spanning two worlds.

Take a moment to find a quiet place.

Reach your arms out as far as they can go.

If you're standing, your body will make a T shape.

Stretch your right fingertips as far to the right as possible, straining to graze some invisible target. Let your left fingertips span as far to the left as possible. Feel your arms pull in opposite directions. Notice the muscles engage in your back and shoulders. Notice the expansion of your chest.

Take a few breaths in that position. Breathe from your core, right from your belly button.

Take in the strength of your arms and the expanse of yourself. Take in how much space you can traverse. Take in how hard it is to hold your suddenly heavy arms in this position longer than a few seconds.

Also notice how open and vulnerable your heart is in this position. Your throat and your chest are unprotected.

This is your life now. Big reach. Reaching almost past what your body can bear. Reaching to be strong and expansive with an unguarded, vulnerable heart. A heart that can feel the full range of the human experience.

It isn't comfortable to be this stretched out and this exposed. But it might be the only way to move through grief with both joy and tender sadness. It might be the only way to hold loss and love together within one heart. It might be the only way to avoid getting stuck in grief or bypassing it all together. It requires so much strength and courage to exist this way. You're spanning two worlds: the world of the living and the world of the dead.

You can do it. I know you can. I'm here with you.

Fire, Water, and the End of the World

I GREW UP in Redding, California. It isn't what non-Californians think of as California. There are no beaches and no tech companies. It is mostly mountains, forest, and lakes.

My entire childhood, I was very aware of fire. Every year or two, lightning would strike a tree in the dead heat of summer, and a fire would demolish thousands of acres of forested land. The Sacramento River Valley, in which Redding is situated, would fill with smoke. And if the fire was really big or close to the city, ash would choke the air and cover the trees and the cars, the whole world, with a thin gray film.

My dad took fire safety very seriously. Our family went camping every summer. He seemed most at home cooking out in the open and sleeping in a tent. We drove west over the mountains to Humboldt County to sleep among the redwoods and play bravely in the very, very cold Pacific Ocean. Or we'd drive south to Santa Cruz or north to Crater Lake. Sometimes we'd just drive an hour or two from our house—somewhere near Mount Shasta or Burney Falls.

No matter where we went, camping days began and ended with a campfire.

We children were taught fire safety as soon as we could walk. My parents camped with us even when we were babies.

Now that I have children, I understand what a tremendous feat that was. I really have no idea how they pulled off the logistics, much less the safety of keeping three young children from breaking arms or getting burned.

There were lots of instructions about fires. My dad was a fire master. He built campfires with the care and technique of someone orchestrating the launch of a space shuttle. There was protocol and order. There were proper materials, steps that must be taken in a specific way.

As we got older, we each earned the high honor of being the fire assistant. Stacking the wood just so—my dad was an aficionado of the teepee method. As fire assistants, we were permitted to add a log to the fire. The addition could be made only when requested by Dad, and the log must be placed in exactly the right spot. My dad was ever watchful. After age eleven or so, we had the right to have our own fire stick. This coveted privilege consisted of using a long stick to poke the fire intermittently throughout the evening. I'm not sure that it served a deep purpose, but it was a rite of passage in our clan.

After my brother Dave finished high school, he joined the California Conservation Corps. For several summers he and his team were tasked with supporting the firefighters who worked Northern California's summer forest fires. They cleared brush and dug ditches. The also tended back fires to choke off the fire's access to dry forest fuel.

My brother, like my dad, was a fire master.

My family was also a water family. We spent our Saturdays at Whiskeytown Lake, situated in a beautiful national forest, twenty minutes from our house in Redding. My dad had a special spot where we went almost every summer weekend. "The spot" from my childhood was a picturesque little beach, reachable only by scaling down four hundred meters of steep terrain. We'd hike up and down "the mountain," transporting all the stuff for the day's adventures. My mom would walk down slowly, using her cane and a raft oar to steady her steps.

My parents started going to "the spot" shortly after they moved from Indiana to California as a young married pair in their early twenties. It was at "the spot" that they decided to name me Sherry. I imagine my mom lounging in the cool lake on a hot August day with her beautiful round tummy peeking out from the water, perhaps my dad floated in an inner tube nearby. The two of them, young and beautiful, accompanied by their dog, dreaming about their soon-to-arrive first baby.

My dad was intense about Lake Day. There was a process, a protocol that must be followed to ensure that we would be the first to arrive to get our choice spot and that no piece of necessary lake equipment be overlooked. Sunscreen, towels, rafts, toys, dog shampoo, jugs of water, picnic food, hats, Wiffle balls and plastic bat for water baseball, a tarp for shade, beach chairs, and his snorkeling equipment—every item was packed and unpacked with military-style orderliness into the giant blue beach bag and loaded into the family minivan. We'd depart the house before 8:30 a.m. most summer Saturdays.

It was a nightmare for me when I became a teenager. Getting up at 8:30 on a Saturday morning was rough. The regimen was rough. I was not overly thrilled to follow my dad's meticulous schemata. The sunscreen must go in the left side pocket. The towels must be trifolded to optimize fit. Fill the blue water cooler one-third full with ice, the remainder with water.

I'm a mild slob now, and I suspect it is unresolved teenage rebellion rooted in Lake Day.

It wasn't unusual for my brothers and me to venture far out into the lake on an inflatable raft, our golden retriever swimming alongside us. We made up stories about pirates and sea monsters. We entertained the possibility of great white sharks lurking in the water beneath us.

My dad would put on his snorkel and fins and do his best to sneak up on us. He'd shoot water out the top of the snorkel, thrilling and terrifying us with his sea monster antics.

Those were my favorite times with my family. It was where I learned to love natural beauty and to value the strength and endurance of a healthy body. My brothers and I came to see the lake, the forest, and the mountains as our playground. Our games involved piling rocks and climbing trees and retrieving lost treasures from deep in the water. It was the place we went to relax, to have adventures, to pass the hot summer days in the cool shelter of the water.

The last time Rob and the children and I visited my dad was July of 2018. He was so sick by then that he spent twenty-two hours a day lying down. But he rallied his energy for a trip to the lake. He got himself into the water and dove in for a last swim in the place that he'd loved his entire adult life, the cornerstone activity of family togetherness.

On July 23, 2018, a few days after we returned to Minneapolis from that last Lake Day, the California weather was extraordinarily hot and windy. A fire started when the rim of a vehicle's flat tire caused sparks to ignite the drought-ridden brush. The Carr Fire raged out of control for thirty-eight days, destroying 1,604 structures, burning 229,651 acres, and causing almost $1.7 billion in damage. Eight people died. Dramatically, the local news station was evacuated during a live broadcast because a firenado with winds over 143 miles per hour swept into the city limits and jumped the mighty Sacramento River. It was otherworldly.

Every tree around that beautiful lake burned down. "The spot" was reduced to ash.

I returned to the lake four months later, during death week. Everything was still black. The trees were gone. The remains of burned houses sat on their charred lots.

The community was still reeling.

And in a parallel process, I was reeling. My grief was only just beginning. I was being forced to say good-bye to the world as I knew it. I was losing my dad. I didn't expect to lose the lake, but now I see it as fitting that we would lose its beauty too. The joy of my childhood was perishing with my dad.

Two days before my dad died, the smell of smoke returned to the air. A firestorm was swallowing up the town of Paradise, California, one hour away. While we were watching my dad leave our lives, eighty-five people were burning to death and tens of thousands of people were left homeless in another monster fire.

Paradise was burning.

My dad was dying.

The world was ending.

The morning of my dad's death, Dave and I drove out to the charred lake. Although the area was not technically open for visitors, we ignored the signs and walked around "the spot." We cried together. In a rare expression of intimacy between adult siblings, we held hands. It broke both our hearts to see the place we loved most as children reduced to a mess of dead trees and ash.

It was an apocalypse. Everything we'd known and loved felt like it was being destroyed.

Exactly one year after my dad's death, I returned to "the spot" and added more ashes. The ashes that I left belonged to Dave, my brother, and to my dad. Their ashes mingled with the ashes of the trees and the brush and the wildflowers. As I stood there the year before, holding Dave's hand and crying about the burnt forest and our dying dad, I could not have fathomed that in such a short time I would be saying good-bye to him too. That he would become part of the charred remains of our favorite childhood memories.

One night, shortly after Dave died, I had a dream about the fire at the lake. In the dream, I was running down the steep hill toward the shore. The fire was just steps behind me. I had a baby in my arms, my baby. I tumbled as I ran through the forest, and when I came to rest, I scrambled under a log embankment and huddled like a scared wild animal.

Then, in the dream, I started screaming at myself like a wild woman: "Get to the water! You can't stay here." I scooped up my child and ran. I stumbled and scrambled, and then I ran some more. Down the hill. Through the trees. In the smoke. I couldn't breathe and I couldn't see and I was absolutely terrified. I felt the fire at my heels, as if it was coming for me, chasing me. Trying to claim me too.

But I ran and I ran and I reached the water.

As I plunged into the lake, I remembered my dad with his snorkel. I remembered that my dad taught me how to swim and how to breathe underwater. I grew braver and calmer, and I flipped on my back and swam with my baby on my belly. Breathing. Floating. Keeping us both alive.

In the dream, I had a deep assurance that I would survive.

I would survive because my dad taught me how to stay safe near fire and how to breathe in water.

take a moment . . .

I came away from the dream with a deep sense that my life had equipped me with the resources I needed to walk through so much pain. Specifically, my dad taught me the things that I'd need to grieve him, because he'd taught me how to work safely with powerful life-and-death forces—fire and water.

Take a moment to meditate on the possibility that everything you need to navigate this pain is already inside of you. That doesn't mean you don't need external support and love, but it does mean you can tap into the fullness of who you are and all that you've learned during all the moments of your life leading up to this point.

It all matters now. The mundane lessons. The special places. The traditions and rituals that were formal or informal. With a little departure from the space-time continuum, you can receive help from the one you've lost.

My dad wasn't perfect, but he gave me what I needed to survive without him.

Practice moving from lostness to assurance. *Everything I need is already inside.*

Search your history, search your stories for the analogies, the strengths, and the lessons that might be helpful now.

Here are some suggestions for drawing out your own inner wisdom:

- Write down key experiences that shaped who you've become. Reflect on those old lessons and consider how they're helpful now.

- Look to the stories of your family or the shared cultural stories that you love. Epics like *The Lord of the Rings*, or sports movies, and other hero's journey kind of stories. These stories often hold helpful collective images or metaphors that are relevant during deep loss and crisis.

- Grief is a good season for a dream journal. Your dreams may hold important narratives that can help steady and encourage you. They are another entry point into your storehouse of inner wisdom. If you aren't someone who has access to memory of your dreams, notice which memories or stories you're drawn to in the early morning or right as you're falling asleep. Where does your mind go in the liminal spaces? When we are between waking states, we are less in our prefrontal cortex, our executive mind. We let ourselves fall into a less defended zone of existence. Perhaps a more spiritual state.

Observe and listen to the wisdom of your own mind, your own history, your own family.

You've had your own lessons about surviving fire and water. *Everything I need is already inside.*

Pants Optional

MY DAD PLANNED to die at home, the home he lived in for thirty-five years.

A hospital bed took over the space where the recliner used to be. I moved the furniture around and made the tearful Target run for extra-long twin sheets and the softest blankets I could find.

Dying at home sounds idyllic. I imagine fading peacefully to sleep surrounded by adoring loved ones. Compared to any hospital I've been in, it is *much* more comfortable to be surrounded by familiar sights and scents and the normalcy of a machine-free living room.

It was comfortable for us too. I'd much rather spend the dying week in my childhood home than in some strange hospital with crap food, terrible decor, and the intrusive presence of strangers.

But let's not tell a fairy-tale story. It is tough business to care for someone at the end of their life. There's very little peaceful sleep for anyone in the home. His breathing was so raspy and wet. It scared him. It scared me. It was the undeniable sound of death.

Neither my mom nor I slept much that last week. It was strange for her when he moved out of the bed that they'd shared for so long. It was strange for me to be sleeping in my childhood room without the assurance that my strong, protective dad was in the room next door, on the other side of the wall, keeping me safe.

He was in the living room in a strange bed with those strange sheets.

He would cry out with pain intermittently throughout the night. I'm not really sure what hurt. It wasn't like any other sickness I'd ever seen. I've cared for people with broken bones or recent surgeries. I've cared for people with stomach flu and migraines and strep throat. In all those things, there is a body part that hurts—a knee or a throat—something you can point to.

At the end of cancer, everything hurts. And it hurts ferociously. It hurt him when I tried to adjust him in bed. It hurt him when I grazed his arm. It hurt to swallow, to breathe. It hurt to continue being alive.

When I had newborn babies, I remember being hyperattuned to their breathing, to the rhythms of sleeping and waking. Rob and I carefully tracked the intake of fluid and the elimination of waste. In their earliest days, our waking thoughts revolved around their sweet, precious little bodies. We stayed up, watching their little chests rise and fall.

Caring for a dying person was very much like having a newborn. Everything is focused on the details of the body. One of my ears was always listening for a cry, a cough, or some sign that the body might be in distress. There was a lot of sitting around punctuated by small flurries of activity. It was sad and painful, but there was a sweetness to it that left me with a deep knowing that this work was sacred and important. It was very tender.

I kept teasing my dad that he was going out like he came in: whiney and needy. I said that when we worked to help him sit up. When he needed me to hold the straw to his lips. When I patted his mostly bald head.

Like most people, he didn't want to get to the point where his family members were helping him wipe his butt. He didn't want the diapers. He didn't want the indignity of that. No one does. That's where the infancy analogy becomes deeply uncomfortable for everyone. In the last few days, he was too weak to stand alone. We worked out a system where I'd help him up, and my mom would hold the pee jar in place. I kept my eyes at shoulder level. I'm not squeamish, and I would have helped him with any part of it, but I am 100 percent happy to say that we got through the ordeal without me ever needing to handle my dad's genitals.

It was a gift to have that little piece of dignity intact.

"I'm not wiping your butt, Dad."

My sardonic humor served to soften and normalize the harsh reality of losing all the acquired skills and dignities of adulthood. There is no ego in death.

Pants are optional.

But it is also true in the deepest, most profound sense, he is going out the way he came in.

Held, attended to, cared for, loved.

May we all be so lucky.

Yoga with Dad

DURING THE DYING week, I went to yoga every day, sometimes twice a day.

It was the best way I knew to practice expansion. To concentrate on breathing and reaching and stretching and holding and letting go all at the same time.

One of the young women who taught me yoga during that week lost her house in the Carr Fire. Her mom also lost her house. Her dad also lost his house. Her whole family was financially demolished by their own battle with fire.

She and I connected over the special art of balancing on a mat drenched in tears and sweat. We connected over the need to practice, to move, to balance—not for the body but for the soul.

During the dying week, I lifted my dad, helped him move, rubbed his neck, listened to his breathing, placed droppers full of medicine onto his lips, and responded to his pain.

By this time, he weighed less than I. He and I wore the same size sweatpants. Cancer left him skinny and weak, and I felt like an awkwardly inflated giant next to him. Cancer brought about an undoing of the order of things. His body was supposed to be bigger and stronger than mine.

My entire life, he'd lifted weights and been a strong, muscular athlete, the kind of dad who used to launch me six feet across the swimming pool. He used to lie on the floor of the living room and bench-press my entire body. He could wrestle all three of us kids at once.

When I was a child, I saw him as a giant tree. Solid and strong and capable of withstanding anything. Dying was undoing all of that. His body had become fragile and childlike. A blade of grass.

During yoga, I kept thinking about how his body lived on in me. I'd stand in Mountain Pose and connect to his broad shoulders. When in Warrior, I connected to the stable, strong legs that held him up. I was deeply aware of our shared genetic makeup. My shoulders, his shoulders. My muscular legs, his muscular legs.

I am made from the same material that he is. My mom is petite with a narrow frame. I'm a good six inches taller than she. Although we share many traits, I have my dad's body: muscular, athletic. Broad shoulders. Quick reflexes. Fast-twitch muscles. An innate kinesthetic intelligence that made us both great athletes. A body that doesn't like to be still. A body that loves a good competition. A body that wakes up early and is ready for action. A body that falls asleep by 10:30 or 11:00 p.m. no matter what kind of interesting activities might be lingering into the night. My son Fisher is built like us too.

I also have my dad's eyes. Hazel eyes with big flecks of blue that can take on different shades in different light—sometimes blue, sometimes green, sometimes gray. The color of my eyes is one of my favorite things about myself. They were an unintentional gift from him.

We are made from the same stuff.

That last week I felt like I brought him with me to yoga— not literally but spiritually, metaphysically, genetically. His shoulders. His balance. His muscles. The genetic imprint that passed from his baseball-playing, motorcycle-riding, waterskiing, weightlifting body into mine.

And so it will be for the rest of my life. Wherever my body goes, whatever my eyes see, a piece of his body goes too. His eyes will see too.

And that brings me some comfort.

take a moment...

Spend some time looking at your body. Your hands. Your feet. Your arms. Notice the details of your skin—the freckles and small scars that decorate you. Notice the shape and length of your fingers.

In his powerful work *The Body Keeps the Score*, Bessel van der Kolk explores how traumatic memory is held in our bodies.[1]

I also believe that our strength and resilience are held in our bodies.

Spend some time thinking through all the stories your body has lived. The moments of pain and the moments of pleasure.

Spend some time thinking about the generational stories that your body carries. The traits passed down, like eye color or fast-twitch muscles, and also the experiences of immigration or famine passed down through genetic memory.

The cells contained within you are a treasure trove of resources. They hold your history, your deepest pains, and your most powerful strengths.

Take a moment and gently massage your hands or apply lotion to your feet. Honor this container of skin that holds you. Anoint your cells as precious and sacred.

The Last Day

MY DAD DIED on a Saturday afternoon. November 10.

It was an elegant ending, as far as endings go. He died within twenty-four hours of my two brothers arriving home. He waited for us to be together.

In the morning, the hospice nurse visited and explained that the time frame had shifted to hours. I didn't know how to gauge the time, so I was grateful for her clarity. She said simply, "He will die today."

Today. Today is the day. Today he will die.

I was generous with the morphine. There was no point in following the dosage guidelines. The minute he seemed uncomfortable, I gave him more. I was in charge of that, in charge of easing his pain.

In the final moments, I was propped up on one arm next to him in his bed. My mom and brothers held his hands. My sister-in-law, Christy, was with us.

He stopped talking around noon. His breath transitioned from rattling and wet to slow and shallow. He stopped working so hard. The room felt calm to me. His preferred cancer-comfort playlist played quietly through his phone.

There were a few heaving breaths, and then I could see a milky fluid in his mouth. My instinct was to reach in and clear it out. But I did not.

It was dark—it must have been approaching sunset, or maybe it was just cloudy outside.

About the time I became aware of the darkness, the noise stopped. His breathing stopped. The fight stopped.

And it was quiet.

He was still.

As he took his last breaths, his beautiful bright eyes became milky, and the color faded. I don't really understand why that happened. Why does death change one's eye color? Maybe I'll get around to looking that up sometime.

There were lots of details that I saw and heard and felt as I watched him die. Details that I will never forget, not as long as I live.

All those details don't need to be recorded here.

Because death warrants its own sacred space. Privacy.

He died in the presence of others. Which is, to me, profoundly brave. He was a private person for most of his life, even with his children. He was not one to show pain or vulnerability. The fact that he allowed us to be with him was very surprising. But I am certain it is what he wanted—what he was waiting for.

We loved him well right up to the very end. We did our best to comfort him, release him, reassure him. We did our best to walk him to the edge, to the place where we could no longer accompany him. And then we let him go, gently, with a wave and a kiss.

I am so proud of him.

And of us.

take a moment . . .

What beauty was present in your loss? What will you hold as sacred?

I will never forget the holiness of the moment that my dad died. The dim light, the soft music, us gathering around to lay hands on his body. I felt an encounter with God, with liminal space, with the other side of the living world.

It stunned me that something so painful could also feel so sacred and profound.

Can you find a sacred moment in the loss? The moment of stillness when breath stopped. The moment when life passed to death. Even if the loss was scary or traumatic, can you find a trace of something beautiful, elemental, spiritual?

If noticing the beauty in death is a stretch right now, maybe there have been moments when you've felt your heart swell to be overwhelmed with love or gratitude or delight? Or moments when you've surprised yourself with your calm or wisdom or capacity for patience?

Don't forget those moments.

Grief is not just the hard moments. It isn't just the sadness.

Don't forget to notice the things that you're proud of.

Don't forget to celebrate the elegance and grace that can coincide with these transforming experiences.

I'm so proud of the tenderness that was present in my dad's last moments. Each of us in our own way surrounded him with such love and deep kindness. It was the best of us.

There's a Dead Body in the Living Room

WHEN THE HOSPICE people first arrived to give us information about the process of dying at home, they brought a list of funeral homes. I called around and did some comparison shopping for cremation services. I am my father's daughter, and my dad loved a good bargain. And really, it is a pretty utilitarian service: pick up dead body from living room, transport dead body, insert dead body into some kind of furnace, collect remaining ashes, return said ashes to the bereaved in a plastic-lined cardboard box.

I went with the cheapest one.

After my dad died, his mouth sagged open. It looked very odd to me, something about the angle was off, undignified, so I reached up and gently closed it by lifting his chin. As I removed my hand, his jaw fell open again. It was both sickening and funny at the same time. My family and I were still gathered around him, and the moment was tender and reverent, but his noncooperative jaw was becoming very distracting for me. I tried one more time to gently close his mouth. Once again it fell open in the oddest way. After the second failed attempt to close his mouth gracefully, it suddenly struck me as very, very funny. Snortle funny.

I surrendered the decorum of sacred death and began to move his jaw like a ventriloquist with a puppet. His jaw moved in sync to my silly voice proclaiming, "Bye, guys! Real good death party. Catch ya on the other side." It made my mom laugh.

Dead bodies are super weird.

He turned glassy and white quite quickly.

About thirty minutes after he died, I called the prearranged, lowest-cost funeral home, but they didn't answer the phone. After another hour or so had passed, there was still no response. I called the hospice to report his death, and they also began calling the lowest-cost funeral home.

The hospice worker was quite worried about this. She really didn't want us to experience having my dad's dead body in our living room for hours on end. I didn't ask much about her specific concerns, but I trusted they were valid.

Each of us took a few minutes alone with his body, and then I covered it with a sheet. The mouth thing was still really bugging me. It was his mouth hanging open in that strange, creepy way that made me feel that he was actually dead. If it was some kind of sick prank, there's no way he could have willfully held that jaw positioning.

There was still the problem of the nonresponsive lowest-cost funeral home. After more calls, the hospice worker finally called the not-lowest-cost funeral home in town and negotiated for them to retrieve the body for the same price as the lowest-cost funeral home. She must've been a good negotiator because, really, they could have doubled their fee and we would have had no choice but to pay it. The body needed to be removed from the living room one way or another. I'm not sure we had it in us to stuff him into the back seat of the Prius.

After all of this back and forth, a rotund man arrived to collect my dad. I don't mean to be unkind, but I was struck by his stature for several reasons: 1) I wondered if the task of moving and burning bodies all day was causing him to stress eat; 2) I wondered if working with death had helped him to so fully accept his own mortality to the point that he was like, "Fuck it, I'll have that third Twinkie"; and 3) I wondered how someone who appeared so unfit was going to be able to handle moving my father's corpse out of the living room. I stared at him in a very unadult way as I pondered these burning questions.

The hospice staff were very astute about which details were most important to tell us. They recommended that we not watch the funeral home staff remove the body. They said that it can be a little jarring. After my experience with my dad's jaw, I understood why. Dead bodies are not cooperative, and no one wants to see the dearly departed being yanked and tugged and shoved into the back of a windowless van. It isn't anything like the loving graceful send-off we'd just experienced.

Somehow the girthy employee of the not-cheapest funeral home performed the mysterious physical feats necessary to load my dad onto a gurney and into the back of the van. And off he went.

I spent the rest of the night rearranging the furniture in the living room.

We woke up on November 11, and the scene of the death was gone.

take a moment ...

Have there been moments of humor in the midst of loss?

A new appreciation for the awkwardness of bodies?

A mischievous moment that lightened the heaviness?

Some well-placed one-liners that cracked open a cathartic cackle?

Look for the sparks of levity and lightness in the darkness of loss. They are there, and they are gifts for you.

The Audacity of the Sunrise

ONE WEEK AFTER my dad's death, I was up, watching the morning sunrise back at home in Minneapolis.

No photo could capture it. There was a new snow, and the vast expanse of white served to amplify every color cast in the waking sky.

I had just arrived home from yoga and was sitting down to write.

My son Fisher was at my feet, working on origami. The rest of my family was asleep under fluffy, warm comforters.

The house was quiet, and Fisher and I were bathed in light and beauty in our little sunroom.

I was often sad during those days. It seems the "slow burn" of cancer doesn't grant an excused absence from grief. Although the cancer journey had helped to disperse the intensity of grief, there was more to be done. Dad's death had opened the door to a new layer of grief—a realization of finality was only just beginning.

It was perfect that it was winter, because grief is best observed in the kind of still quiet that deep winter offers. As a Californian transplanted to Minnesota, I've grown to love the rhythms of cold and warm, new life and falling leaves.

The sunrise moments are what convince me that all will be well. The moments of brightness and newness as I sit alongside my young son. It is these moments that fuel the power to walk through the darker, sadder, scarier experiences. They are moments of light and hope and life that counterbalance the winter of death.

My list of worries was long. They were not the worries of an anxious mind, a mind that needs worry to feel awake. No, my worries were the worries of love. The joining of my hurting heart with the hurting hearts around me. Death caused a void that necessitated the remaking of everyone else. My mom's life must change without my dad. My brothers and I are reorienting, beginning to rewrite our timelines based on my dad's exit from the narrative. Everything must be reworked. The worries must be held tenderly, not "treated" or analyzed or pathologized.

I was worried about my mom. Where should she live?

I was worried about my brother Dave. I knew he was desperately sad. But there was a distance growing between us. I felt like I couldn't reach him.

I was worried about my brother Dan. His quietness meant I was never quite sure how his heart was faring.

I was worried about my children and their burden of having a mother who is sad, who has been away so much.

I was worried about my husband and the sense that we'd lost some of the sweetness and ease with which we'd lived most of our life together.

The business of being remade is sacred and messy, and worry is a fair by-product.

I longed for quiet and stillness to sort through my busy mind, but I lived a life in motion: full of voices and the thumping of small feet up and down stairs.

My vocation is to engage deeply with other people's stories. My mind is full of listening, of attuned presence.

There was no monastic cave to crawl into. My life could not stop for long.

So I continued the journey of expansion—of holding grief and worry alongside life and joy.

The sunrise is my teacher in this.

It emerges from darkness with a slow, gentle motion. It seems to respect that the darkness has its place. Its emergence is not aggressive or defiant. Yet it does not for a moment deny itself. It does not apologize for the brilliant display of light and color. For the act of entering into the aliveness of day.

Nor will I diminish my aliveness by lingering too fully in the land of grief.

take a moment . . .

Most of us don't get much time to be still after a major loss. There are problems to solve and things to do. We go back to work and jump back into our caretaking responsibilities. Email the team, drive the carpool, outline the project, pack the boxes, organize the event, make the phone calls.

If you could choose, what combination of motion and stillness do you most need right now? Is there a sense of being rushed into action or forced back to "normal life" too soon? Or are you ready to celebrate the aliveness inside you that counterbalances the weighty sadness of loss?

There's no right answer. But there is wisdom in checking in with yourself each morning. Notice when you may be longing for space and quiet. Notice when you need to feel the beating of your heart and the action of your body and mind.

Grieve accordingly.

Live accordingly.

Binge-Watching Is My Transitional Object

AFTER MY DAD died, I started falling asleep to *The West Wing*.[1] I moved a TV into my bedroom, and when I woke up in the middle of the night, I would turn it on and watch until it was time to get up or until I fell back to sleep.

In some strange way, Martin Sheen's character, President Jed Bartlet, was a transitional object for me. He helped me bridge the gap between a world in which I had a father and a world in which I did not.

My dad wasn't the presidential type, and I'm pretty sure he never voted Democrat—so the connection to the fictitious Jed Bartlet wasn't direct or based on their shared politics. But like Jed Bartlet, my dad had a strong moral code, was committed to his faith and his marriage, and was a "try to do the right thing" kind of person. He was reliable, and he kept his word. My dad was also flawed and limited and ill—something that could also be said of Jed Bartlet. He was a complicated person to look up to.

In a very simple, childlike way, I simply slept better with the thought that Jed Bartlet was watching over things.

When I was a child, I often woke up with bad dreams. The combination of a vivid imagination and a deeply empathetic awareness of the world did not make for a well-rested childhood.

As I began to learn to soothe myself in the middle of the night, most nights I just had to remind myself that my dad was on the other side of my bedroom wall. He was in the next room. Even without calling for him, his presence was instantly comforting. I knew he would help me and protect me and chase away the monsters.

Watching *The West Wing* into the wee hours of the morning was an odd attempt to grasp the same feeling. The feeling of a safe, helpful, protective presence standing by.

A transitional object is usually a stuffed animal or a blankie that helps a young child make the emotional jump into a new level of independence—the shift from a crib to a big-kid bed or the switch from preschool to kindergarten. A transitional object helps soothe upset emotions and is sort of a partner on the hero's journey into unknown autonomous terrain. *The West Wing* was my transitional object. It provided comfort and company as I shifted from a person with a father to a person without a father.

I don't remember when I stopped falling asleep to *The West Wing*. There was no intention or ceremony around it. I just stopped doing it one night. Perhaps I was too tired to turn on the TV or just decided to watch something else. However it happened, I don't do it anymore. I've relearned how to sleep without the protective presence of a parental guardian.

Don't Rush

I HAD A traditional wedding: a church, bridesmaids, cake, veil, flowers—the full deal. Rob wore a tuxedo with tails and a white bow tie. I wore a dress with lots of pearl beading and a fabulously long train. We were beautiful together. It was our prince-and-princess day, a day I will eternally remember as one of my favorite days ever.

My dad walked me down the aisle in my long-trained gown.

As we began to walk, he whispered to me, "Go slow. Savor it. This only happens once."

I think about that moment a lot now. *Savor* is one of my favorite words. I like how it feels when I form the word in my mouth. I love what it means.

My dad taught me to love things enthusiastically: the 49ers, golden retrievers, motorcycles, the #32 combo plate with chow mein from the Chinese place on Placer Street, the feel of cold lake water on a quiet Saturday morning, the scent of redwoods, BBQ sauce.

My dad didn't live a perfect life. There are many sad stories and heartaches that I didn't record here. But he was pretty good at finding happiness despite hardship and setbacks. He lived simply, and he lived with contentment.

He savored.

He wanted to stay longer, to keep living for many more years. He valued the moments of his life and wanted to fight for them. He wanted as many moments as possible.

I'm savoring things for both of us now. Sunsets and snuggles. Long walks with the dog. The simple delights that add up to a satisfying life.

And that's a legacy I'm determined to carry forward.

It's a legacy I'm grateful for.

I tried my best not to rush as he walked me down the aisle on my wedding day. I tried to match my steps with his. I tried to be present to the moment and let myself feel it, all of it: the bliss of walking toward my awaiting soon-to-be husband, the radiance of a room filled with all the people that I loved, the steady presence of my dad next to me.

I'm trying not to rush. I'm trying to walk slowly through this grief phase of my life, as if the grief is walking right beside me, in sync with my steps. I'm trying to notice the moments when my heart longs for my dad. I'm trying to tenderly nurture the hurt and let it be part of me. Going slowly seems like the best way to savor him and all that he was to me.

Go slow. Savor.

Okay, Dad.

take a moment . . .

It is impossible to extricate grief and love. They are intertwined like light and shadow and roots and plants. You can't have one without the other. I am in grief because I was in love.

That is what makes grief a beautiful expression of strength. It is not an enemy. It hurts because it *should* hurt.

In your messy moments, when it is hard to get out of bed and you feel like you're cracking open and certain that your insides will spill out, please remember that grief is love. That all the pain you're holding is an expression of the immensity of your love. It is its own treasure.

When the grief becomes too dark, too much, love is the counterbalance.

Seeking the love of the living is an important part of grief. Hugs, phone calls. Letting your community know that the loss of love is painful and you need a little extra love to fill that void. Don't accept the messages of "stiff upper lip" or the pressure to move quickly into some version of resilience. Let love pour in from as many sources as you need. Go slowly through grief so that you can absorb all the love that is offered to you.

When you feel empty, consider a focused breathing practice in which you inhale and exhale a flow of love—your image of love is cycling through you as your body moves air in and out. Perhaps that love feels warm and bright (like a hug or a smile). Perhaps it has a color. Perhaps a scent. Imagine the sensation of love filling you from your nostrils to your belly button. It flows in and out in the shape of an oval, warming you, lighting you from the inside out.

This is not disparate from grief. You can weep and be full of living love at the same time. You can long for the one that is gone and also accept the gifts of the ones that are here.

You can revere and savor this pain for what it is: the deepest expression of your loving heart.

PART THREE

suicide

The Obituary That Was Never Published

THIS IS THE obituary that I wrote about Dave.

It was never printed. I didn't have the heart to put it in the paper, and at the time of his death, my mom, Dan, and I wanted privacy.

It felt too painful to release it into the world.

But I wrote it anyway. For us. For my mom and Dan and Rob and my kids. And for me.

I also wrote it to honor Dave.

> On May 10, 2019, David Jeffrey Muterspaugh departed from this life.
>
> Dave was born in Redding, California, on May 14, 1985. He spent his childhood playing baseball with his dad and siblings and falling in love with the mountains and lakes that surrounded him in Northern California.
>
> He battled an addiction to alcohol for most of his adult life. For the last two years he was alive, he fought hard for his sobriety despite numerous setbacks and heartbreaks. He succumbed to his struggle on a sunny spring morning steps from Glacier National Park in northern Montana.

Dave loved natural beauty. He worked and played in the Whiskeytown National Recreation Area; Lassen Volcanic National Park; Big Sky, Montana; Yellowstone National Park; and Glacier National Park. He was a river raft guide, cross-country skier, cycler, kayaker, and back-country hiker. He had a deep respect for wildlife and a desire to protect the wild spaces that gave him so much joy.

One of his proudest achievements was solo biking the 1,000 miles from California to Montana at the age of twenty-two.

Dave also loved to cook and loved to play music. He had a gentle spirit and was helpful and kind. He may have been too tender for the world in which he found himself.

His homemade salsa was second to none. And his omelet was king.

He is survived by his son, Gage; his mother, Marcia, of Redding, California; his sister, Sherry, of Minneapolis; and his brother, Dan, of Sacramento. He will also be deeply missed by his brother-in-law Rob; nephews, Fin and Fisher; niece, Genesis; sister-in-law, Christy; and numerous friends in California, Montana, and Minnesota.

He was preceded in death by his father, Tim.

take a moment . . .

Do you need to write an obituary? A simple summary of the existence and departure of the person, ability, or thing that you've lost?

A failed business, an illness that's changed your independence, a divorce, the death of a pet—sometimes a simple summary of the presence and subsequent loss can be a cathartic memorializing. Obituaries don't have to be limited to dead people. And even in that case, you may want to write your own version of the obituary, not simply roll with the version that Aunt Ida gave to the newspaper.

The obituary you write may be very different from the one that was printed in a public place.

An obituary is a simple summary. Begin with the basic facts: name, dates of beginning and ending. Then note a few big highlights. Add some personalized descriptors. And then list the names and relationships of those deeply affected (the "survived by" section). You can also add an in memoriam section. Perhaps you want to add some instructions to yourself—in lieu of flowers, I will make a chocolate cake and share it with someone I love.

It feels good to get it all down.

Dave Is Going to Die

APRIL 16, 2016, was the first time that I confronted the harrowing thought: *Dave is going to die.*

It was Dan's wedding day. Our family was gathered in Stinson Beach, California, to celebrate Dan and his much-loved new wife, Christy. Friends and extended family had come from the Midwest and all over California for a beautiful ceremony on a hill overlooking the Pacific Ocean. It was a perfect day: the weather cooperated, their dog was the videographer, the reception was beautiful and perfectly complete with ice-cream tacos, which my children consumed delightfully unsupervised.

We all had a role to play. My youngest son carried the rings, wearing red high-tops and refusing to tuck in his dress shirt. My oldest son played the cello during the ceremony. I was the officiant. Dave was a groomsman.

Despite this delightful backdrop, it was the day that I began to know that tragedy was lurking.

I suppose Dave really began dying the moment he started drinking. His relationship with alcohol began as an occasional contraband beer with a friend in his high school punk band, or a cold one with his older brother after a long hike. It seemed like normal, nonchalant exploration of alcohol and autonomy and gentle teenage rebellion.

However, for some reason, alcohol took hold of his adolescent brain with a force that dictated the course of his life. By the time high school graduation rolled around, he was drinking every day. He dabbled with other drugs over the years, but alcohol was his go-to.

He lost things. He made bad decisions. Formed no college plans. Struggled to keep jobs. Had mysterious car accidents.

Right after high school he paired up with a woman who was also abusing substances. They got pregnant.

Dave cared for his baby with such tenderness that I had a glimpse of hope that their young, unlikely family might work out.

But there was darkness there—drug use, constant alcohol consumption, fights between Dave and his girlfriend that turned ugly and aggressive. It quickly devolved into a mess, and Dave moved out.

His new reality became accumulating child-support debt and difficult negotiations with the addicted, angry mother of his son. No meaningful work opportunities. It felt like his life was over before he'd had the chance to get started.

With a broken heart and deep shame for failing as a father, he set out for Montana on bicycle.

He made a new life in the mountains. He worked restaurant jobs while he trained to be a river raft guide.

He loved the guiding work, but three summers into the job, someone drowned in an accident on the river. Dave was not involved. It wasn't his raft. But it scared him, and he stopped working on the river.

He spent a summer camped out in a meadow. I wasn't clear whether that was by choice or because he was homeless. Years passed. He shuffled between jobs. He seemed mostly happy and always had wonderful adventure stories to tell.

But when Dave arrived in Stinson Beach for Dan's wedding, he didn't look like the wild, adventurous mountain man of his stories—he was swollen and yellow. He had a pouching belly that didn't fit the life of someone who spends hours a day on a bike or a pair of skis.

In the midst of the wedding day's morning chaos, Dave snagged a hangnail on the side of his finger, and it started to bleed. He wrapped it in tissue, and we continued our prewedding preparation frenzy. We sat down to go over the wedding details one last time. We had lunch. We put on our wedding best.

As we prepared to leave for the ceremony, I noticed a little drop of blood on his shirt. In big-sister fashion, I escorted him to the bathroom and used hydrogen peroxide from the first aid kit to get the little spot off his dress shirt.

As I reached down to throw the peroxide-soaked tissue into the bathroom trash, I saw that the bin was full of blood-soaked tissues. It was a lot of blood for a hangnail. He'd been bleeding for hours.

I knew then that something was very wrong.

"Your blood's not clotting," I said. I looked him in the eyes, and he looked away. I repeated what would become a mantra from me to him: "I'm worried about you."

It started with a hangnail.

It started with one beer.

I suppose it always starts in a small way. Every explosion begins with a spark. Every tornado is born from a wisp. The path to destruction begins so quietly, often with the soundtrack of a "normal" family playing in the background.

The worst thing is that I saw in his eyes that he didn't care. He was unconcerned about his own yellow, bloated, bleeding body. Unconcerned that a small wound had been bleeding for hours. And it was the first time that I felt like I couldn't really find him. He sat right in front of me, his hand in my hand, but I couldn't reach him, I couldn't touch him. We were living in completely different realities, and my words, my face, my pleading couldn't penetrate the fog that moved in his mind.

I began practicing for the possibility of Dave's death on Dan's wedding day. Perhaps my knowing was just intuitive, perhaps it was based on the years of clinical training that had shaped my mind. I saw the risk factors. Whatever guided it, it was clear and real, and it lodged in my mind that day and never went away.

I knew that Dave would die. And at the same time, I had no idea.

How do you know something with depth and certainty and yet find it to be completely implausible?

I have hundreds of memories of us playing together: riding bikes, throwing a baseball, running through the sprinklers in our yard, eating popcorn and watching whatever kid movie was on TV, swimming in the lake. We shared ten thousand meals at our family's dining room table. We argued. We teased each other. We frustrated each other.

In all that time, all those thousands and thousands of hours growing up, side by side, I knew him as someone who was happy. His mind was sound. He heart was kind. He was playful and loving and irritating in the ways that all little brothers are to their big sisters.

How is something absolutely unthinkable and perfectly predictable at the same time?

The only way that I can describe it is to say that the brother I grew up with slowly, gradually, got lost. We were tethered together by the bond of genetics and shared history and family, but the years of alcohol and distance frayed the tether. And by the time I recognized how far away he was, it was too late to do much about it except sit beside him while he fought his inner battle.

I used to know him. And then slowly, over time, I didn't anymore.

The part of me that knew him could never imagine this as his outcome. This wasn't how it was supposed to go for the mischievous blue-eyed boy staring at me from behind the breakfast cereal box.

But the part of me that recognized his lostness, that saw the stranger emerging in him, felt instinctually that this lostness was very, very dangerous.

When I got the phone call that Dave had died, I fell to the ground in shock. But if I'm honest, I'd been preparing for that call for years.

take a moment ...

Most of the people I know who have lost a brother or sister or son or cousin to addiction, experience some kind of premonition. Addiction and mental illness are a slow burn, but the unraveling is punctuated by moments of poignant, shocking clarity.

As you look back on your loss, are there ways that you "saw it coming"? How does your sense of premonition shape the loss for you?

Does the "knowing" help? Does it help you feel more mastery over the story to see how the pieces fit together?

Or does the knowing become a tangle of responsibility and helplessness?

This is a difficult part of this story for me. The "knowing" decreases the loudness of the shock, but it also creates a sense of helplessness and responsibility that weighs on me heavily. Like watching the unfolding of a car crash, I saw the series of events unfolding, and I knew they could create disaster, but there was nothing I could do to stop it. No one heard me yelling.

In the world of Western psychology, this kind of "knowing" is often attributed to hindsight bias. It seems that humans tend to retroactively see events as having been predictable. Most traditional psychologists argue that hindsight bias is a kind of memory distortion.[1] We feel the "knowing" only at the end of the story, only after the disaster has imploded in front of us. Hindsight bias is the brain's attempt to protect us from the unpredictability of the world. *I knew that was going to happen* protects us from the randomness of tragedy and the pain of our exquisite vulnerability. Our brains take comfort in patterns and predictability.

Seeing the through-line in the sequence of events that caused your loss might be helpful to you. It might help you see how the pieces fit together to form a cohesive story. It might help it make some sense. Dave died in an instant, but he had been dying for years, and that perspective is important to counterbalance some of the shock.

But be careful about how this retrospective clarity hooks you into a feeling of knowing, when, in reality, you could not really have known. It is entirely possible that the story could have gone another way. Be gentle with the part of you that is grasping for predictability and clarity. Be gentle with the part of you that was holding out hope for a different outcome.

Angels in the Zombie Maze

MY PREMONITION BEGAN to take shape on Valentine's Day in 2017.

That was the day that my dad learned that the cancer in his body was not isolated to his esophagus. He learned that there were tumors in his lungs and lymph nodes. We all learned that the cancer was very, very serious. Dave went into a tailspin.

My dad and I had returned to my house after a day spent at the Mayo Clinic, and my mom met us at the door with a wildness in her eyes. She'd had a phone call from Dave's friend Holly and learned that Dave was in the hospital in Montana.

The story was confusing. He was drinking. He hit his head. He vomited. He fell down.

It sounded like a bender that had ended badly. Maybe a concussion and some stitches.

I didn't really understand.

I called the hospital in Kalispell and was eventually transferred to a nurse named Christina. She used words like *aspiration*, *organ failure*, *brain swelling*, and *medically induced coma*. It felt like she was talking about someone else, like she was recounting the story of some other patient.

My head cleared enough to ask the real question: "Is he going to die?"

She responded, "It is an hour-by-hour situation."

I left for the airport.

It was late at night when I landed in Kalispell. I quickly learned that there were only two Uber drivers in the greater Kalispell area. The wait was an hour because there was a party in Whitefish and *all* the Uber drivers were dispatched to the shindig up north. I called the hotel to see if they could recommend a cab service or had another transportation idea. To my surprise and delight, the Hilton Garden Inn offered free shuttle service anywhere within the Kalispell city limits. Ten minutes later, the hotel shuttle driver picked me up and drove me right to the hospital. He took my things to the hotel and told me he'd come get me anytime, even 3:00 a.m.

In the coming weeks, I came to know the shuttle drivers well. There were two of them—they doubled as maintenance and hotel support staff when they weren't driving. One driver was young, with young children. We chatted about sleep training and marriage when your life is full of toddlers. The other driver was older and semiretired. I liked him best and ended up riding with him most often. When I asked, he told me stories about his lifetime spent living in the mountains. He was gruff and slow to warm. But we spent a lot of time together in the van, so he seemed to soften to me. He drove me back and forth to the hospital every day for weeks. Sometimes at odd hours. He let me sit and cry in the back seat when it became too much. He talked with me when I felt lonely and wanted a human conversation.

There are no set visiting hours in the ICU, family members could show up anytime and stay as long as they liked. That first night I arrived around midnight. I followed the signs and walked down long, dark deserted corridor after long, dark deserted corridor. Hospitals are strange places in the middle of the night. I didn't pass another human in those long hallways. It felt like a postapocalyptic movie where everyone else had been killed, or raptured, or had run off to hide in the woods. By some sick twist of fate or theological error, I was the only one left.

Maybe in the entire world. I had the urge to run down the hallways as fast as I could, to get under cover, to escape the zombie that must be slowly trudging after me. I felt oddly exposed.

After wandering up and down the maze of the deserted hospital, I found the ICU. I had to ring a buzzer and state my business to the invisible person on the other end of a shiny black camera. "My name is Sherry. I am David Muterspaugh's sister. I am here to see him." The invisible cameraperson worked some wizardry that produced a buzzing sound. The locked doors opened before me. Another long hallway, but this one had the distinctive ICU soundtrack of beeping monitors and rhythmic machines pumping and dripping and doing whatever magical medical thing they do in the night. Eventually I encountered an actual human sitting behind a desk. It was almost startling. It seemed off script after what felt like hours meandering the lonely maze.

The ICU in the middle of the night is a place of hush. I had the impression that I was supposed to whisper. There were only a few staff. And the patients were quiet, except for their machines.

Entering my brother's room was a new chapter in the evening's apocalyptic narrative. Dave had so many machines and tubes and straps connected to his body that I could scarcely find a patch of recognizable skin to kiss. There were trickles of blood down the side of his face. There was dirt and blood caked on his hands. His wrists were fastened to the sides of the hospital bed with thick white cotton restraints. His head was bandaged and seemed to be held in place with another cotton strap. Most of his face was covered with a breathing mask. There was a tube down his throat. There were giant compression boots on his legs that reminded me of astronaut gear.

He looked like a highly technological version of Frankenstein's monster. Maybe after the monster returned from a failed mission to space.

I moved a chair to sit as close to his head as I could. And then I started talking to him, like in the movies. You're supposed to talk to people in comas, right? In case they can hear you.

"I'm here," I said. "Your sister is here. It's me. It's Sherry. I'm here, Dave."

The truth is, I wasn't talking to him for him. I was talking to him for me. We were on the edge of reality, in the desolate land of mazes, machines, and zombies. And it was just him and me, alone in this apocalyptic world. We were the only survivors, and he was my only human companion—even though he was in rough shape.

I have no idea what I talked to him about. Probably Netflix or the lack of Uber drivers in Kalispell or my kids' latest music performance or our parents. Inane stuff.

Some part of me believed that if I bored him or irritated him enough, he would wake up, roll his eyes, groan, and kick me out of his room. That he would sit up and take off the ridiculous Frankenstein astronaut costume and say, "Just kidding, Sherry." And then I would be mad and yell at him for making me fly all the way to fucking Montana and letting me get scared in the abandoned zombie hospital.

Of course, I wouldn't stay mad, and we'd laugh and go eat pizza.

But he didn't wake up, and I got tired of talking. I pushed the magic black button that beckoned the other awake human, and I asked for some clean towels. I soaked the towels in warm water and rung them out in the hospital room sink. I tenderly wiped the exposed skin on his face and his hands. I tried to get the blood off, so that he would look more like himself. Perhaps so that he would remember that he was not a zombie or a Frankenstein monster.

I gave no thought to having contact with my brother's blood. I know it's not an ideal choice from an infectious disease standpoint. But his blood is my blood. I'd been patching up his scrapes and cuts since I was eight years old.

I had to be careful of all the tubes.

I did my best to wipe away as much blood as I could. And then I left the dirty, wet, bloody towels in what looked like a laundry bin, and I kissed the back of his hand.

It was about 3:00 a.m., just as my shuttle driver had predicted. I steadied myself, called him to pick me up, and began meandering the long maze to the front of the hospital where he arrived to collect me. Though we'd met only once, a few hours earlier, I was deeply relieved to see his familiar face. It felt grounding to climb into the back of the hotel van and let someone else worry about driving. I let myself feel tired.

For the next week, I camped out in the ICU. I got there early in the morning to be in the room when the doctors made their rounds. I sat around for most of the morning and left midday for a workout, a meal, a nap, and a shower.

I listened to music. I did a little work. I sat beside Dave. Chatted to his silent body. Tuned out the machines.

Besides the drivers, the ICU team became the other most important people in my life. I knew them all by name. I met Christina, the nurse from the phone. I came to know the pulmonologist and the neurologist. I learned about their hobbies and their kids and their schedules.

For each of the five days that Dave remained in a coma, there was a different worry: brain swelling, pancreatic function, fluid in his lungs. It wasn't until the third day of my encampment that the doctors began to feel confident that he would live. I did my best to endear my brother and myself to them. I asked thoughtful questions. I told them stories about Dave and his life. I saw them as his bridge between staying mostly dead and coming back to life.

The team decided to "wake him up" after five days of sedation. We planned it so that I would be there. Dials were turned, drips were adjusted, cotton straps were removed.

He slowly began to shift around and make some groaning noises.

Eventually he roused, confused and agitated, like someone had interrupted a long nap.

But he knew me right away. Our blue eyes locked in brother-sister knowing. "I'm here, Dave. I'm here."

As the medication began to clear out of his system, he became agitated and confused. He tried to pull out the many tubes still assisting his body. I tried to explain not to touch them. I tried to move his hands. I tried to play him calm music. I tried to distract him. But he was not my little brother anymore. He was a grown man, bigger than me, and he was not interested in listening to my sage advice. He pulled super hard on his catheter and started to scream.

His disorientation was really upsetting to me. I started to cry. Nurse Christina came in and surveyed the chaotic scene. One screaming sibling. One crying sibling. I'm sure my mom can relate. Christina reassured me that it was probably not within my power to reason with Dave in his current state. The restraints went back on. She told me that this kind of disorientation is normal. She put her hand on my shoulder. It was one of the most important moments of human touch I've ever received.

Dave had a long road. But there were people here to help.

The only reason he survived is that he was thirty-one years old, and his body was determined to override his destructive mind. He spent four weeks in the hospital.

As he began to heal, it was clear that he was motivated to stay alive. He kept asking to borrow my phone to call random friends. And as I predicted, he asked if we could order a pizza.

On my last trip to the hospital, the older driver picked us both up—Dave and me—and drove us back to the Hilton Garden Inn for one final night. The driver was beaming when he met Dave. He'd been following his story during the many car rides we'd had together over the course of almost a month. The driver was such an important part of those weeks for me. Picking me up, dropping me off. I began my day with him and ended it with him. He navigated the snowy streets with calm and confidence. And he always asked if I needed to stop at the store or run any errands. He delicately turned up the radio any time I started to cry in the back seat. He was consistent, reliable, and kind. And I can't remember his name.

But I'd give him a kidney if he needed one. He helped me when I was desperate for help.

He drove Dave and me to the airport four weeks after the first night he had picked me up. He gave both of us hearty hugs. I kissed him on the cheek and tearfully thanked him.

take a moment . . .

Were there surprise angels in your story? A nurse, a driver, a smiling woman behind the coffee counter?

A Delta ticket agent once personally retrieved my luggage from a delayed flight so that I could take another route. There are surprise kindnesses in most of our stories if we look for them.

Jot down their names (if you know them) and short descriptions of how they helped you.

If it feels right, perhaps send a thank-you card. Or leave a five-star review. Or just send up a prayer or thought of gratitude.

Let your heart linger with these helpers for a moment. Feel their care. Feel your connection to them. Soften into gratitude.

The driver and the nurse named Christina were my angels. Their actions weren't extraordinary or valiant, but they gave me a gentle sense of belief, of confidence, that I could find kindness and help when I was most in need. They were the answer to the prayer I didn't know to pray. A whisper of grace.

Merry-Go-Round of Horrors

EIGHTEEN MONTHS AFTER the Kalispell ICU, much of the story repeated itself.

I found myself in intimate contact with my brother's blood. Wiping his hands with warm hospital towels.

A different hospital in a different state. This time it was the Hennepin County Medical Center in downtown Minneapolis.

I got a call from someone at the hospital switchboard. I got another call from the manager of Dave's apartment complex. I got another call from the ER staff.

I was the emergency contact on all the forms, and this was an emergency.

Again, there were fragments of information. They found him in the stairwell. Transported by ambulance. Multiple stab wounds. Maybe self-inflicted. Blood transfusion. Immediately to surgery.

I spoke to a nurse. I spoke to a physician. I asked the same question, "Is he going to survive?" Once again, the vague answer. "We'll know more in the next few hours."

I got in the car.

And once again, I entered a hospital room to find his body bandaged, restrained, and buried in tubes. It felt less like science fiction this time. The reality of this story didn't take so long to sink in.

After his time in the Kalispell ICU, Dave had returned with me to Minneapolis. Within a few days of his arrival, my dad (who was in Minnesota for his Mayo Clinic workup) and I dropped Dave off at an inpatient addiction treatment program. Thirty days, sixty days, ninety days. He could stay as long as he needed. He stayed for six months. And he did well.

We all knew the stats about treatment and relapse. This was his first attempt at treatment, and he was determined to take back some of the power that alcohol had wielded over his life. After being in an inpatient program for six months, he transitioned to a partial day program. He lived in a sober house and started the weekend shift manning the omelet station at Hotel Minneapolis. There were lots of ups and downs. But he did well—went to therapy, worked the program, took the medication. He rode his bike all over southern Minnesota. He spent hours on a paddleboard.

Then my dad's cancer moved into his brain, and his death became imminent. And the tether to my dad tugged on Dave in some mysterious way. He began to struggle. He was in and out of the ER for strange bike accidents: a broken collarbone, a concussion, a fractured wrist.

One August morning, I found him in my kitchen making breakfast. I wasn't expecting him. He looked up at me and said, "Did you know that Dad died?" And he started to cry.

But my dad hadn't died. Dave was confused and disoriented. Maybe intoxicated. Maybe overmedicated. Maybe having a psychotic break. Maybe experiencing some kind of brain injury. I couldn't tell.

I wasn't surprised when, a few weeks later, I received a call from an emergency room physician saying that Dave had been brought in with a giant gash on his head. I pleaded with her to keep him in the hospital for a full evaluation. I told her I was afraid that he would kill himself either accidently or on purpose. I explained that he'd been in and out of the hospital and that he seemed disoriented and confused. I told her his history and asked her to do a full medical workup to see what might be causing the confusion. Based on my request, she asked a judge to place Dave on an involuntary hold, meaning he couldn't leave the hospital and that the hospital had the ability to hold him in a locked unit.

The locked psychiatric floor of a major urban medical center is a horrendous place to spend time. When I visited, I had to surrender my phone, my keys, all my personal items. I could bring him snacks, but they had to be sealed and undergo inspection. There were two locked doors, and I had to buzz in to each one after identifying myself: "My name is Sherry. I am here to see my brother, David Muterspaugh." It was plain walls and metal—no framed art with glass. It was very much like the jails I worked in after I graduated from college. I was scared to be there. I can only imagine how he felt.

Dave knew that I had advocated for him to be hospitalized. He wasn't happy with me. But he wasn't angry or unkind. Rage and blame were never his thing.

He stayed for several weeks and then once again went to a treatment center. To try again.

He stayed until the beginning of November when our family began death week. I called the doctors, spoke to the clinic directors, and asked that Dave be released to come back to California and say good-bye.

I took so many actions in that season of his life: advocating for him to stay in the hospital, asking for him to be released early. People listened to me because I have a PhD and I am articulate. The truth is, I don't know if those actions were right. I don't know if the hospital broke his spirit even more or if being with my dad when he died was too much for him to take. I don't know if I should have stayed out of it. Or fought harder for different treatment centers or different timing. There have been moments when I have berated myself for those choices. There have been moments when I wish that I'd done different things. Or done nothing.

But I am sure that in all those moments I did what I did because I was trying to love him as best I could. Trying to protect him, trying to help him, trying to connect with him. Trying to help him stay alive.

It was February 2019 when I once again asked for towels to clean the blood out from underneath his fingernails. My dad had been dead for several months.

Physicians and their teams can perform medical miracles by applying space-age superglue to a ripped-apart windpipe and elegantly reconstruct the arteries in the forearm, but they don't bother with the bloody fingernails. That is the sister's job.

Once again it was my face he saw when he awoke and realized he wasn't dead. It was different this time. We sat together, noticing his mixture of relief and disappointment.

He didn't ask to borrow my phone. He wasn't in the mood for pizza.

When he tried to speak, he had to use a bandaged hand to apply pressure to his trachea. His voice came out raspy and weak—like a broken squeaky toy.

My baby brother had stabbed a knife through his throat and into his wrists. I have no idea how sad and angry and hopeless you have to feel to be able to do that to yourself.

One of the worst moments of my life was calling my mother.

How do you share this news with your mother? My sweet, kind mother who was still writing thank-you cards to people who helped with my dad's memorial service. My sweet, kind mother who would have made an extraordinary first grade teacher had multiple sclerosis not truncated her career. My sweet, kind mother . . .

It was the last phone call I wanted to make in the entire world.

It wasn't eloquent. I was probably kind of detached and clinical—shutting down my feelings.

She had to come out and ask me, "Was this a suicide attempt?"

Apparently, my first explanation was vague on the details.

"Yes, Mom. Yes. He was trying to die."

take a moment . . .

What was the worst moment? The low point? No one likes that question, but it is an important one.

When we use psychotherapy to treat trauma-related problems like PTSD, the low-point question can be key to the treatment process.

Often it isn't what you think. Sometimes the phone call is harder than the blood.

Finding the courage to wade into the memories in search of the low point is extraordinarily difficult. But it is also the key to healing. The low point tells you what you're healing from, specifically.

My low point tells me that, although I am working through the loss of my brother, I'm also healing from the loss of myself. I lost a piece of my identity, my ability to see myself as helpful, protective, and competent. I lost my ability to protect my mom.

Find the low point, the true low point *for you*, and you'll more clearly see where you may be vulnerable to getting tangled in grief. It is often the part that is hardest to reconcile.

It Could Be Me

I LOST A friend to suicide in June of 2020, a little more than a year after I lost Dave. His name was Michael. He was my officemate during my postdoctoral fellowship at the National Center for Posttraumatic Stress Disorder in Boston. Michael and I shared a closet-sized office for a year as we worked under the same principal investigator at our elite research-training center. Our office was so small that I had to pancake my stomach into my desk so that he could squeeze by me and sit down at his table.

Michael was messy and brilliant. He was a statistics genius and, therefore, a highly sought-after conversation partner for the many other researchers and fellows on our hall. He knew everyone and graciously introduced me to the community of aspiring academicians that made up the cast of characters in our professional lives.

He was my "better half" at work. We collaborated together, joked together, covered for each other, reminded each other to get the articles from the printer. We traded books, took turns picking the soundtrack for the day. We shared many lunches together and occasionally had family dinner in each other's homes. We took turns journeying down the long VA hallway to refill both coffee mugs.

For that year, he was one of the most important people in my life.

His death was shocking.

Michael had a dad who had a multiyear battle with cancer.

Michael had a brother who battled mental illness.

Michael had a very successful career—he was a well-loved professor.

Michael had two beautiful children.

Sound familiar? Michael and I shared overlapping heartbreaks and overlapping stresses and overlapping joys.

Michael's death reminds me that none of us are exempt from the potential to die like this.

Death by suicide increased by 30 percent in the United States between 2000 and 2016.[1] And those numbers don't account for the tremendous negative impact of the global COVID-19 pandemic.

There are lots of opinions as to why that's happening. While we're on the subject, I'll add a few of mine:

The United States has been sending people to combat in the Middle East for roughly the same period of time. Approximately 20 percent of people who die by suicide are veterans, but they make up only 11 percent of the US population.[2] War drives some of the increase in suicides, but not all of it.

Social media became a pervasive part of life during that time. It has redefined human belonging into emoji and tallies of likes and hearts. Twitter rants have replaced thoughtful conversation. Impostor syndrome and FOMO are now cornerstone experiences in a culture that interacts in sound bites and highlight reels. We're now all comparing our lives to a filtered, curated, highly fictionalized version of everyone else. We're inundated with people information but lonelier than ever.

The cost of medical care skyrocketed between 2000 and 2016. Health care is increasingly hard to navigate and pay for. Many mental health professionals (myself included) do not work within the health insurance system because it is far too time consuming for the relatively low reimbursements. This means that many highly qualified and experienced mental health professionals are only accessible to the wealthy who can afford to pay out of pocket.

But most of us aren't patient enough for a lengthy course of psychotherapy or spiritual direction, or even the time required to work with a psychiatrist to find the right medication regime.

Instant access to information and answers via Google, Siri, and Alexa make us a "right now" culture. Everything happens in real time. There's not much practice for "wait it out, try again tomorrow." Our distress tolerance is low.

Which brings me to medicine. We are a drugged-up culture: pain medication and a pervasive use of psychotropic medication directly contribute to the rise in suicide rates. We feel a feeling and we want to zap it with a pill.

I'm not antimedicine, but in most cases, medications can't solve all the problems we want them to solve. I've seen medications save lives—more than once. And I've seen them accelerate someone's undoing—more than once.

People are lonely and hopeless and ill and want those feelings to go away fast.

I know all about those feelings. I have them too.

Maybe some of the problem is the absence of black mourning bands. Our culture has become excellent at selfies but unable to tolerate pain. We have no cultural rituals around sorrow, at least none that last longer than a weekend. We celebrate our beauty but rush to quickly suppress and conceal our pain.

We are expected to bury a parent on Saturday and attend the board meeting on Tuesday.

Where does that leave the tender hearts? Where does that leave those who are grieving or depressed or feeling like their world is spinning out of control? We've left no place for them.

Michael was self-reflective and open. He talked with me from time to time about the pain that he felt. His sadness and grief. We shared many tearful phone calls over the years. I'll never know what shifted within him such that he felt unable to manage the extent of his pain.

As with my brother, I just wish he'd chosen to stay.

take a moment . . .

Trauma and loss can cause a "foreshortened sense of future." [3] Loss can stop time, stop imagination, stop dreaming. It can inhibit our mind's ability to imagine any kind of life on the other side of pain. Really, this is the essence of posttraumatic stress disorder: the mind and body become stuck in a trauma story and can't reground itself in a safe world. The belief that pain is permanent and unchanging is a very real risk factor for suicide.

Getting stuck in pain is a real experience, and one to be cautious of and to protect against. It is one of the reasons that working with a therapist is helpful. A skilled clinician can help you enter and exit the intensity of your pain and can help you shift if you begin to feel too stuck.

When we fear that we will get stuck in our pain, we run the risk of overcompensating in response to the danger of stuckness, and we close down our openness to our pain. We push it away and hold it at arm's length.

Our collective mental health would be radically improved if we could practice experiencing deep pain and grief without fearing that we will get permanently stuck in those dark places. Our cultural aversion to grief leaves us believing that it is dangerous and that we shouldn't give oxygen to the anguish inside of us.

It is unaddressed anguish that becomes dangerous.

Grief, trauma, and loss distort time. Wading through requires us to build some time-traveling skills. I talked about timelines and orientation to place and time earlier in the book. I now want to add another dimension to our ability to navigate grief across time. We need to flex our capacity to imagine the future.

What will be happening in your life one month from today? One year? Five years? Ten years? The questions aren't just annoying prompts for English class. Our ability to envision our future self has an important protective power for mental health and for all future-oriented life decisions. The capacity to imagine the future draws from a capacity to hope. It is incredibly important in navigating trauma and grief and, specifically, in reducing risk of suicide.[4]

Let yourself imagine your way into a different era of your life. Your power to envision change over time will help prevent you from feeling stuck in the permanence of your current pain. You've not always lived in grief. You won't always feel your grief in this way. It will change.

In your rough moments, consider placing your current anguish in the context of the past and present. Something like this:

PAST	PRESENT	FUTURE
Five years ago, I was camping in Oregon with my cousin and her dog. It was miserably hot, so we spent most of the day floating in the lake. I remember the cool water. We talked all day.	Today I am struggling to get out of bed. It is a shame day. I feel bad about feeling bad. I am sad. My hair is a mess. Nothing is interesting. I miss my dad.	Five years from now my youngest son will have just turned sixteen. He will be taller than me. I can't wait to see what kind of young man he's becoming. I wonder if he'll still be blond.
One month ago, I worked a full, busy day. I was productive and helpful. It felt good.	Today I am angry and grumpy. I've been short-tempered with the kids. I feel ugly inside.	Next month on this date, I will be in Portland for a conference. I will be in professional mode—wearing nice clothes and talking with colleagues.

It is a simple practice, but one that makes concrete the
movements and phases of your life. You've been somewhere
else before. You'll be somewhere else again. Today is what it is. If
you're miserable, accept that. But know, in your bones, that it
isn't permanent.

When Lifelines
Become Entangled

DAVE WAS ALREADY on a destructive path before my dad was diagnosed with cancer.

But my dad's diagnosis ripped him wide open. Every time the cancer took a turn for the worse, my brother entered a new level of destruction.

Within twelve hours of our dad's death, Dave filled himself with liquid morphine and liquid lorazepam—stolen from the supply provided to my dad by the hospice nurse—and went looking for alcohol. Within twelve hours of Dad dying, Dan and my mom and I were wondering if Dave was also dead.

Eventually I located him in the county jail.

I don't know why my brother couldn't picture existing in the world without our dad. I will never understand why their fates were so closely intertwined. They didn't seem enmeshed or oddly codependent. My dad encouraged and respected Dave's autonomy. Dave had no deep need to linger close to home. From the outside it seemed like a healthy, supportive relationship between a father and an adult son. For some mysterious reason, their lifelines became entangled. As soon as it became clear that my dad would die, my brother also seemed determined to die.

This isn't unique to him. Recent bereavement elevates risk for suicide. Suicides often happen in clusters within a family, school, or community. People experience a desire to join their lost loved one. They're overwhelmed with sadness and the logistical burdens that go along with continuing life without someone who is deeply integrated into their existence. Knowing someone who has died by suicide seems to put suicide on the menu, even in minds where it wasn't previously under consideration.

Grief is an extraordinarily fragile time.

This pull toward death among the bereaved was confusing to me when I learned about it in graduate school. Wouldn't an experience with death make you long to be alive? Wouldn't it make you want to run as far away from death as possible? It seemed counterintuitive that the death of a loved one could pull someone toward more death.

It wasn't until Dave died that I understood how grief can draw you toward death. In the weeks and months after his death, I had trouble sleeping. As I lay in my bed, exhausted and feeling alone, I felt myself slip into a deathlike place. My thoughts turned to Dave, and I wondered about him and the possibility of his existence on the other side of the veil. I talked to him in my head. A mixture of sadness, anger, and yearning:

> *Take me with you, little brother. Take me with*
> *you to the place of darkness and quiet. Don't leave*
> *me alone here with our shattered family. And our*
> *sobbing mother. Don't leave me here alone.*
>   *Let's slide down together. I'll join you in*
> *the dark, and we can decompose quietly*
> *into the nothingness.*

It wasn't until Dave died that I could empathize with an all-consuming heaviness that made death feel like a reasonable plan for the relief that I so desired.

Grief brings death so very close. This unknown mystery becomes palpable, tactile. The delusion of invincibility is shattered, and death becomes possible and familiar.

I've spent a lot of time thinking through Dave's last morning alive. What was his state of mind? Did he plan to die on the six-month mark of our dad's death? How long had he planned this specific route of departure? I imagine him riding his bike and getting off and leaning it against the outside of the small simple structure of the remote mountain train station. He sets down his backpack. He sees the train coming. He stands up.

I walk it through in my mind. And when I do that, I walk with him, I stand with him. I can see what he saw and feel what I imagine he felt. It is the worst side of empathy.

I haven't had lots of conscious suicidal thoughts in my life, but this empathetic imagining means that the prospect is no longer so foreign to me. My mind has practiced walking with him.

My hunch is that Dave felt some of that:

My hunch is that my dad's death opened Dave to an intimacy with death. Perhaps he replayed our dad's death in his mind too. And came to imagine the steps and see the ending as a welcome reprieve.

Seeing someone die is profound. The last breath and the complete settling of the body. The stillness and the quiet. In my dad's case, it was eerily beautiful. I wonder if it was inviting to Dave.

In the Harry Potter books, thestrals are creatures that are invisible to most people.[1] The first time Harry sees them, he is afraid that he has gone mad—he is clearly seeing something that others are not. His friend Luna explains what they are and why he can see them. Thestrals are imperceptible to all except to those who have seen death. Her explanation eases his distress. Luna can see them too. He is not alone in having witnessed someone depart from life. He is not alone in knowing exactly what death looks like.

Once you've seen death, you see differently.

I see the thestrals. And my brother saw the thestrals. I wish I could have helped him to be less afraid of them.

Or maybe less enamored with them.

take a moment . . .

What does it mean for you to be someone who has known death? How has it changed you?

Does death seem familiar, even comfortable, like a companion that your mind knows well? Does it loom scary and impending, like the image of the monstrous reaper lurking in the shadows? Are you intrigued, enamored, curious?

Without judgment, notice the quality of the relationship that you have with death. Notice the emotions, the words, and the images.

Explore writing about death. If death were personified into a human or animal form, what would it look like to you? What images does death bring to your mind? Try to describe them. Perhaps play with poetry or nonlinear writing to express what death is "like."

Express with art. What colors or forms give a visual dimension to death? Is it darkness and shadow? Is it blood red? Is it a claw breaking through the ground? Is it a tender angel?

Sketch, paint, or use another visual medium to express the familiarity you have with death. You may also consider compiling images from magazines or photos from online.

Explore expressing death through yoga or movement or dance. What shape does it take in your body? *Savasana* (Corpse Pose) is the part of many yoga traditions in which the practitioner explores nonbeing, in which we practice feeling death in the body. Or maybe your expression of death is more active, more chaotic, more fraught. Could you dance through the feelings of death or hold a snapshot of death as a pose with your body?

The intention in this exercise is to move from vague impressions, tendrils of fantasy, into a more personalized and cohesive impression of what death is to you. Your personal version of thestrals. Giving shape and description to an abstract, powerful force helps our brains have a clearer sense of whom or what we are dealing with when we encounter death.

The Autopsy in My Inbox

I WANTED THE autopsy report.

I wanted to know.

I wanted to know where.

I wanted to know how. How exactly.

I wanted the information that could help me bridge the distance between his aliveness and his deadness. Facts functioned like stepping-stones to guide me from one reality to another reality.

A reality in which Dave is dead.

I filled out a form that I printed from the Glacier County Sheriff's Department website. I took a photo of it with my phone and emailed the pdf to the sheriff's office.

A woman called me. An assistant sheriff, or sheriff's assistant, I'm not sure about that. She said, "I'll send it to you, but you need to know that it is not written for you. It is a detailed accounting of the scene. A factual description of what happened. Some of the details in your brother's report may be upsetting."

I received the autopsy report on a Tuesday afternoon. It sat in my inbox. An email like all the others that I am oh-so-slow to deal with. I let it sit there until Thursday night when I'd finished most of my work for the week.

As a professional, I've read lots of incident reports—police reports, military reports, medical records. I'm used to this kind of writing. It is terse and descriptive, probably authored as someone is rushing to finish up paperwork and get home to a kid's T-ball game. The call came in at such-and-such a time and officer so-and-so arrived on the scene. . . The facts. Listed as bullet points in a timeline of events.

Dave was referred to as "the decedent."

There were lots of people involved at the scene of my brother's death: a captain with the Glacier County Sheriff's Department; a Montana Highway Patrol trooper; a member of the BNSF Police (the train police); several representatives from the train company; the train engineer; the train conductor; a tribal officer, a member of the Blackfeet Law Enforcement Services; and an FBI agent (my brother died on land that belonged to the Blackfoot tribe, which apparently means that a federal officer has to be involved).

The FBI relinquished investigatory jurisdiction to the county sheriff.

There are lots of details in that report that I will carry with me for the rest of my life. Details that are hard to know and hard to carry.

Although it is written in a dry, basic, informational way, it paints a picture. His hat lay here, his backpack was found there. The train was traveling at twenty-seven miles per hour. There were two engines. His body was dragged 78.9 feet from where it was struck to where it came to rest.

Everything is reconstructed in the report. Although I imagine the sheriff was strictly doing his job, there are some detailed descriptions that do make it feel human. As I read it, I felt like he was really paying attention and trying to understand exactly what happened.

I appreciate that.

I won't share more of the details here. There's no need to traumatize everyone.

And my brother deserves the dignity of privacy.

But I will hold the details in my mind and in my heart. They are both painful and precious to me.

I shared the autopsy report with my husband, Rob. He asked me to send it to him. He said simply, "I want to know what you know." And I loved that line. He didn't want me to hold the details of the story all by myself. He didn't want me to be the only vessel. And so, he holds it with me.

There is one part of the sheriff's report that was important for me to know. I've quoted it below. The sheriff is describing his conversation with the train engineer and the conductor:

> They stated the male stood in the middle
> of the tracks. They thought, at first, the male
> was playing "chicken" with the train. They
> explained that the male put one leg back
> and brought his arms up and appeared to be
> bracing for impact. They advised the horn
> was sounded and the emergency brakes were
> set, but the male did not move, and they struck
> him. As soon as the incident happened they
> called 911 to report it. Both men reported that it
> appeared to be intentional.

Intentional. Dave meant it. He did it on purpose.

The train conductor had time to sound the horn and apply the brakes. Dave braced for impact. He stood his ground in the face of an incoming train.

It had been so important for me to be with my dad in the last moments of his life. I saw his suffering. I saw that he was ready. I watched his eyes cloud and his breathing become more labored. I knew that he was a little scared, but also peaceful and resigned. I knew that he knew that he was loved. He was surrounded by his children and wife. We went with him as far as we could. Comforting him. Tending to him. Easing his pain and his passage as best we could. The last moments of his life are not a mystery to us.

I got to walk with my dad all the way to the gate and say good-bye and send him off on his journey with a hug. And that made the grief a little easier.

With my brother, there was no send-off. The only witnesses to his last moments were the train's engineer and conductor. He died without touch or comfort. Under metal.

The autopsy is the only link to those last moments. I wanted to grasp at whatever I could to try to reach into the mystery so that I could be with him there.

But there's no report that can teleport my love to him across the expanse of space and time.

The only thing the coroner's report makes clear is that Dave meant it. He was sober when he did it.

And he died in an instant.

The Chapter Where I Grapple with Blame and Responsibility

MY DAD AND I had a conversation a few days before he died.

He gave me the passwords to his phone and his accounts. He talked to me about life insurance and showed me where all the files were. He expressed his fears about what would happen to my mom.

He asked me if I would be okay.

And he asked me to take care of my brother.

It was easy to say yes to the last question. I said yes with my full heart.

After Dave died, I watched old home movies as I put together a slideshow to honor Dave's life. There was one thirty-second clip that told the story of our relationship. He was about three. I was about ten. We climbed to the top of a tall twisty slide at the Sacramento Zoo. He got to the top and glanced down the slide. He hesitated. His blue eyes got wide. He was scared. It was so big for him. He turned back to me, and he curled his little body into mine. Without hesitation, I sat down, scooped him onto my lap, wrapped both of my arms around him, and down we went. In the movie, you can see his face relax and his eyes light up. He loved the slide once he felt safe in my arms. We reached the bottom, and he jumped up and down. Elated. Delighted. The video recorded his little-boy voice screaming: "We did it, Sherry! We did it."

I gave no thought to my dad's question because I'd been taking care of Dave his whole life.

I am seven years older, and our mom's illness impaired her ability to do some of the physical heavy lifting of motherhood. I was half sister and half mother to Dave.

I taught him to ride a bike, to climb trees. I carried him around on my back. I fetched him for dinner. I picked him up when he fell. So interwoven was this as part of my identity that my dad called me Little Momma from the time that I was eight.

I talked Dave through his first love, helped him dye his hair black during his punk band phase. We discussed clothes and girls and how to cope with the ups and downs of living with my parents. We were on the phone for hours every day during the weeks that he was deciding what to do about the unexpected pregnancy.

He lived with Rob and me during the six-week gap between working as a river raft guide in Yellowstone and running a ski lift in Big Sky.

I loved him so much. He brought me so much joy. Almost like one of my own children.

And I felt responsible for him. Right from the beginning, I was trained to be responsible.

"Sherry, keep an eye on David."

"Sherry, hold David's hand."

"Sherry, where's your brother?"

That's why it was so easy for me to introject his life into myself. I've spent my entire life being responsible—tending to the fragile, tender souls around me. From my two younger brothers to my children—biological and acquired—to my students, to my clients.

In psychology-speak, I'm a parentified child. Many therapists are. We're well practiced at discerning the emotional needs of others and responding accordingly. Many of us have been doing this for our primary caregivers since we were very young.

Most of my life, I've seen this role as a deep privilege. I am strong. I am loving. I am not afraid of depth or complexity.

It usually feels good to be useful, to be needed, to have something to contribute.

When Dave was released from the hospital in Montana, I brought him back to Minneapolis with me. I packed up his things and flew with him. I played my role. He couldn't yet walk well, so we had one of those airport carts drive us through the Minneapolis airport. We laughed really hard at the silliness of it. We were siblings in that moment, being playful on the cart in the airport.

I wanted Dave nearby.

I chose to get involved.

He was with us for two years in Minneapolis as he cycled through treatment, then a sober-living house, then an apartment, then back to the hospital, then back to treatment. He repeated that cycle a few times. Many people do. That's the story of addiction and America's shitty mental health system.

I navigated the tightrope of not doing things for him but trying to let him know that he wasn't alone. This was much easier said than done. He'd done quite a lot of damage to his brain with years of heavy, heavy alcohol use. His problem-solving skills were not great. He was easily frustrated and discouraged.

I chose to get involved, and because I did so, I tied my heart to his. Extra tight.

I wish it would have been as easy as scooping him up into my arms and helping him down the slide. But it was so much harder than that. The merry-go-round of loving someone who is fighting addiction is nauseating and absolutely exhausting.

Within two minutes of learning about his death, I began the long and complex set of mathematical gymnastics to try to unlock the answers to how this happened and whose fault it was.

I should have let him stay with me. Live with me. I should have helped him find a better living situation than the shitty, unsafe sober house his treatment program had dumped him into. I shouldn't have advocated for him to stay in the hospital. I shouldn't have expressed anger when he stole the hospice medication and took our mom's van, crashed it, and ended up in the county jail.

I shouldn't have distanced myself so much. I should have dug down deeper and found more love to give him.

These are my sadder thoughts.

As time passes, I find more and more equilibrium in this "should" conversation. There were moments when I could have been more kind, and there were moments when I loved him perfectly.

In the end, I just wasn't that powerful. In the end, I couldn't turn the tide for him. In the end, he alone chose his path.

Sometimes I whisper aloud to my dad, "I tried, Dad. I really tried to take good care of him."

And I imagine him saying, "I know, Sherry. I did too."

We all tried.

take a moment . . .

Loss disrupts so many parts of who we know ourselves to be. We all carry with us old scripts for parts we were taught to play as children in our particular families. This script gets upended when loss or crisis rearranges the family constellation.

There are lots of roles that children are asked to play in a family. Some that are a common part of popular vernacular include: the black sheep or rebel, the baby, the golden child or favorite, the peacemaker (usually a middle child), the achiever (usually the oldest), the comic relief, the savior. Less common are: the ghost child, a child that's born after another child dies; the identified patient, a child that is ill or disruptive, and the family organizes itself around that illness; the parentified child, a child that must take on the role of a parent due to a parent's illness or absence.

I was the parentified child. However, I fired myself from that job when I lost the brother that I was supposed to take care of. Now I'm trying to figure out how to rewrite my role in my family. If I'm not a junior parent, who am I? If there's no baby brother to coddle, what role is there for me to play?

What was your assigned role in the family? How did that childhood role follow you into your adulthood? When you reflect on your story of loss, how do you see yourself playing your assigned role? The responsible one? The peacemaker? The black sheep? The comic relief? The one aligned with Mom? The one aligned with Dad? The baby? The villain? The savior?

How does your journey through loss challenge the roles you've been playing since you were a child?

Did the weight of responsibility become too much?

Is it impossible to become the peacemaker now that the combatants are gone?

Are you lost as to what your place should be? Or are you grateful to be liberated?

Does the loss create space for you to take on a new role? For you to have a better ability to choose how to love and belong among those who are your family?

If you want to dive deeper into this, consider a writing practice like this:

MY CHILDHOOD ROLE	MY ADULT ROLE	HOW LOSS CHANGED MY ROLE
Parentified child, Little Momma.	Caregiver for my parents, brothers, children, etc. Still feel very responsible to support and help others.	I almost drowned under the weight of responsibility to take care of Dave. I don't want to carry that weight anymore. I am choosing to let my remaining family members be responsible for themselves.

Breaking it down like this may help to see the roles more clearly. You may also want to explore what is lost and gained by the change in your role. ●

Ten Thousand Answers, but No Reason Why

WHY?

There is no answer to that question.

And there are ten thousand answers.

There wasn't one thing that caused Dave to kill himself. It wasn't one moment or one situation. It isn't as simple as grief or alcohol or depression. It wasn't his lost relationship with his son or his financial troubles.

It was all of those things.

It was ten thousand moments. Ten thousand things.

His heart broke in little ways for years.

I spoke to him on the phone a few days before he died. He had just returned to Montana, and he was full of love and hope. He texted me photos of the snowy mountains that surrounded him.

The last words that I ever said to him were "I love you."

And that is a moment for which I am eternally grateful.

The worst-case scenario is not that Dave died.

The worst case would have been that Dave died without anyone trying to stop him. Without anyone loving him. Without anyone trying to help him claw his way out of the mess.

I'm glad I showed up for the losing battle.

Not trying is worse than trying and losing.

Even though it cost me dearly, not trying would have
ruined me.

Fuck the happy ending. There were ten thousand reasons to
show up for the losing battle.

take a moment . . .

Notice your "should've." The regrets that punctuate your memory
of your loss.

We all have them. The things that, in retrospect, we wish we
would have done or said. It is okay to have moments of allowing
yourself to wish that events had unfolded differently. Gentle regret
can serve a purpose if it helps us find clarity about how we might
want to adjust our choices, assumptions, or values for the future.

But beware that the voice of "should've" can be harsh. When your
editorial review of your past is chastising, angry, critical, or harsh, it
fails to help you learn, grow, or understand.

I find that my "should've" moments go better when I stop talking
to myself as myself but find the flexibility to talk to myself as one of
my friends would. Or as my dad would.

We're much kinder and more balanced to others than we are to
ourselves. We need to shift our inner monologue. If you can't shift,
or you're stuck in the self-critical regret spiral, that is a good time
to bring in a literal outside voice—a therapist, friend, coach.

When "should've" voices or surges of regret come into your mind,
invite them to the inner table. Listen to them or write them down.
Give them a moment to express themselves. Don't automatically
force them into silence. Let them have a little space.

And then ask those voices to shift from past to future. *What
would you have me do differently in the future? How can I love
better in the future as a result of this experience?*

Here's an example:

One should've that I've struggled with is that I didn't intervene
when Dave felt scared and unsafe at the last sober home he went
to after treatment. The "home" was shitty, and the other occupants

were terrible to him. He felt desperate to get out of there, so he went back to Montana, probably before he was ready for such a big transition. He asked me for a place to stay, and I didn't help him. In retrospect, I understand how desperate he was. At the time, I was honoring a boundary that I'd set of not housing him. I regret that I didn't listen better or try to find a creative solution. In the future, I will be more attentive when someone makes a direct request of me, and I'll be less beholden to the rules that I've set up in my head.

Sitting in "should'ves" won't help you, and it doesn't honor the love that you had for the one you lost. The voice of regret can be a helpful teacher if it speaks with gentleness. And if it is the right time to listen.

I Can't Come with You

THE GRANULES SLIP SO easily through the spaces between my fingers.

Like the sand we played in when we were children.

At the beach.

In the backyard.

It's so much easier than I thought.

To go.

I love you—I said.

I didn't know it would be the last thing that I ever said to you.

Maybe I did know.

There were enough reasons to believe that all manner of destruction could be possible.

I stopped believing it would be okay.

And I was right.

It wasn't okay.

Your departure cracked me open.

I could hardly breathe.

The stitches that held in my own abyss.

Became dislodged.

The gray shadow of death began to fade me beyond recognition.

I withered.

Colorless, lifeless, and still.

Like you.

But I made a different choice.

To stay.

To come back to life.

Maybe for my children. Maybe for our mother.

Maybe just for me.

How do you come back to life?

I suppose it is the same way that you grow life in the
first place.

Warmth, light, water.

I wish I could have given you those things.

I wish I could have helped to revive you.

But in the end, there was only me left to save.

So I spun and climbed and flew and swam.

I lifted and I ran.

I hugged and I held.

And I kissed and I made love.

And I fought. I fought like my life depended on it.

Because it did.

When I remembered what it was like to be alive, I began to
crave it.

I remembered that I loved to sleep under the trees

and swim in blue water under an orange sky.

I wanted to cling to life. To my life.

I couldn't hold on to you and hold on to myself at the
same time.

So I let your ash slip through the spaces between my fingers.

I released you into the water.

I watched you disperse. And float. And sink.

And return to the wild world.

I let you go. Because that's what you asked of me.

And holding on would have been my own undoing.

take a moment . . .

Poetry has been extraordinarily helpful to me in my grief. I'm grateful for emotional, expressive writing without the burden of sentence structure or punctuation.

Reading poetry has also been extraordinarily helpful. Mary Oliver, Rupi Kaur, Rilke, Janne Robinson, Yung Pueblo, Naomi Shihab Nye, Najwa Zebian—these poets have been the soundtrack to my grief, providing comfort, commiseration, and an invitation to find beauty in darkness.

If it has been a while (maybe high school) since you've read much poetry, I highly recommend a perusal of the poetry section in the bookstore or do a bit of poetry Googling. Loss is a common theme among poets, and I suspect you'll find some resonance there.

Poetry is the tapas for the soul. Small bites. Rich with flavor and nourishment.

Death as Light and Feathers

IN HER POEM "White Owl Flies Into and Out of the Field," Mary Oliver explores death not as darkness but as light.[1] Light that is warm and feathery and enveloping. The poem ponders whether passing from this life feels something like being carried away in a moment of amazement.

I love this description of death: the light, the softness, the image of being carried. It stands in such contrast to the typical image of death as cold, sleepy darkness. Or as the enemy of life.

My dad and my brother were both in desperate need of relief. And I hope that ease and gentleness awaited them on the other side of this life.

As my father was dying, I whispered in his ear, "It is okay to let go. It is time. We love you." I believe that those words were important to him, that the words helped to release him. I believe that he, too, longed to be reassured that his work on the earth was complete. The blessing to go seemed to calm his mind and his body.

Dave was also in tremendous pain. It wasn't the pain of cancer, but the pain was tenacious and absolutely overwhelming to his mind and body. One could argue that Dave's pain was different but equivalent.

But in stark contrast to the comfort and release I attempted to offer to my dad, my words to Dave were always things like "Hold on," "Hang in there," "Keep fighting."

I would never have said those things to my dad as he entered the advanced stages of cancer. I knew that no amount of tenacious fighting could reverse the path toward dying. I would never have asked him to do something I knew was impossible simply because I didn't want to be without him.

In retrospect, it seems unkind that I said those things to my brother.

I wish that I'd also been able to tell Dave that it was okay to go. I wish I could have told him that I don't judge him. That I understand. And that I also wanted him to feel some relief.

Those are scary words, aren't they?

If I had said those things aloud, would it have sounded like permission? Like I am condoning or supporting his choice to die? That I agree? Some mental health Dr. Kevorkian?

Permission and choice. They're both illusions.

Did I give my dad permission to die?

No. He was going to die regardless of what I said about it. He didn't have a choice.

My words of release were spoken in an attempt to ease his mind.

Did my lack of permission keep Dave here on the planet?

No. He died regardless of what I said about it.

Clearly I have no power over these matters of life and death. None of us do.

But I do wish that I could have had the moment to give Dave a tiny bit of ease. To whisper in his ear, "I'm sad you're going. I love you."

I wish I could have sent him off in love.

But an open conversation about his impending death could not have happened. I would have begged him to stay. Or I would have used my powers to once again send him to the hospital, by force if necessary. I did it before. I tried to force him to stay, convince him to stay. That is what I did over and over. That is what I'm trained to do as a psychologist, and it was my instinct as a sister.

I didn't listen when he tried to tell me that he needed to go.

Because I believed that he had a choice.

Did he have a choice?

Permission and choice. They're both illusions.

There were no measurable tumors in his body. And we don't yet have definitive scans to assess mental injuries, although it is possible that scientific advancements in coming years will demonstrate a clear link between organic brain damage and suicidal depression.

It is possible that he died of pain and injury, just like my dad did. Dave's cells were broken, too, just a different set of cells.

All I know is that I wish I could have sent him off in love. With a gentle whisper, "Let go. You are released from this pain. You are released into ease."

I like the image of him ascending into light as soft and floaty as feathers.

You'll Never Know Him

I WISH YOU could've known my brother. I wish you could've met him. He was sweet and shy and kind and had the most brilliant, beautiful blue eyes. And the world is a tiny bit worse because he's not here. Not just for me. It's way worse for me, but it's a tiny bit worse for you too.

That is the greatest heartbreak of his death. There are no more chapters in the book. There's no possibility that you'll stop by my house and find him in the driveway, helping one of my children replace the inner tube in their bike tire. You won't meet him on your next RV adventure through Montana. I won't be able to connect you by email after loudly proclaiming, "You're going to Glacier National Park! You've got to talk to my brother! He knows all of the best spots."

His son won't have him in the audience at his high school graduation. My mom won't have him nearby when she needs some help gardening, or when her health starts to fail.

The people who stay at Hotel Minneapolis won't experience his fabulous omelet making. The people leaving a Vikings game won't have him as a pedicab driver.

All those people, all of you, will never have the chance to encounter him.

take a moment . . .

If I could make a humble request of you, now that you have spent
all this time reading, it would be to try to see the people around
you, the shadowy people, the hidden people, the people whose
social media profiles aren't glorious. The people who bring you your
coffee or clear the brush from around your house. The people who
check your ticket or bag your groceries. The people sleeping on the
bench at the bus station.

I plead with you to communicate to them, in whatever method
you have available to you, that they are valuable. That they are
worthy of respect and care. Sometimes a smile and slight nod of
the head are important and sufficient ways to honor the humanity
of another person.

I don't know that small kindnesses would have reversed the ten
thousand hurts that brought my brother to the conclusion that
it wasn't worth continuing the fight, but it feels like kindness is
action in the right direction.

Who around you might need a dose of kindness?

Where are the opportunities, even in your grief, to express love
to a fellow human?

My best hope is that my response to Dave's story will be the
deepening of my heart. And that tender actions and stories and
expressions of kindness will keep him close to me as I go about
my life. And my best hope is that by writing about it, you will
experience a deepening of your heart too. And that you will help
keep him in this life in a tiny way.

PART FOUR

life after death

Metamorphosis

THESE DEATHS AND the grief that has arisen within me have changed every part of my life.

My relationships with my husband, my children, and my friends are different.

My body is different.

I spend my time talking about different things. My work has changed. My play has changed.

I see the world with different eyes.

Name the Ghosts

FOR THE FIRST few months, I hardly spoke about Dave's death. I went about my life: meeting friends for lunch, seeing consulting clients, giving talks, being a professional person, and never mentioning the traumatic death or suicide or even saying his name aloud.

It was like the words couldn't form in my mouth. The few times I did speak of it, the shock on the listener's face was like looking into a sad, horrible mirror. Like the warped mirrors in a fun house.

Some people said thoughtless things and that became too much work to sort through in my mind.

It is such a hard thing to talk about.

At my dad's memorial service, my mom lost her voice. She lost it, and it didn't come back for three months. I began to worry about her. I urged her to go to the doctor. But now I see her hoarse throat as some kind of psychosomatic mercy. She was tired of speaking about cancer and death and her husband of forty-five years. It was time for silence. For a retreat into quiet.

In my months of silence, Dave was never far from my mind. Every third thought was of him. A part of me believed that if I opened my mouth to speak his name aloud, I would never stop.

I would fall down the black hole of grief, and there would be nothing left for me to talk about. Best to seal it off in a corner of myself.

One of the first times I spoke about it, I was on stage at an event in New York. I had just given a talk about mental health and entrepreneurship, and someone in the audience raised his hand to thank me for the talk. He went on to say that he wished more professional events included conversations about mental health because he'd just lost his brother to suicide, and he wished that he'd felt more equipped to talk about mental health. I spontaneously said, "I understand how you feel. I just lost my brother to suicide too." I felt the air go out of the room. It created a concerned moment for the audience. But it also felt right and helpful to say that to him. To join with him in the terrible club of survivors.

When I was a graduate student, I spent the summer in Guatemala to learn how thirty-six years of civil war shape the psyches of individuals and communities. It was a summer of listening to the stories of the bereaved, visiting sites of massacres, sitting around conference tables with human rights lawyers, historians, and fellow psychologists. The trip was so powerful for me that I returned to Guatemala every two years for the next decade, sometimes taking with me groups of my own students.

On every trip, I visited an organization called the Forensic Anthropology Foundation of Guatemala (Spanish: Fundación de Antropología Forense de Guatemala) or FAFG. The team at the FAFG recovers human remains, mostly from rural mass graves, and undertakes the arduous task of reconstructing bone fragments, bits of clothing, teeth—whatever is recovered from the dirt—to try to identify the victims and decipher how and when they died. They can identify the sex and approximate age of the person and whether they were shot, the victim of a blunt-force trauma, or perhaps struck down by a machete. FAFG is a nonprofit organization, and the highly trained staff work for low pay and, depending on the political climate at the time, under death threats. There are many people who don't want the stories of the dead to be told. My first visit was almost canceled because the FAFG had received a bomb threat the day prior.

When you visit FAFG, you walk through several levels of security and then into a small waiting room. Visitors are led down a series of maze-like hallways stacked with boxes, and then enter a large light-filled room full of long tables and computer workstations. It is like an extra-large high school chemistry laboratory but without the Bunsen burners. These tables are for the examination of human bones. Whatever is left after the life has crossed over is removed from plastic bags and piled neatly at one end of a long table. The pieces are then carefully reconstructed, like a jigsaw puzzle, by gowned and gloved forensic anthropologists. They look like surgeons, though their skills are not for saving lives but for recovering the stories of the dead.

It is in this room that I first felt the profound importance of death stories. I felt intuitively, spiritually, that the work of these gowned truth-tellers was sacred and powerful. Many in Guatemala want these cases to remain hidden. They don't want it to be known just how many people were killed—how many children were buried in remote fields—often slain, unarmed, by the hands of government soldiers who were frequently trained by members of the US military.

For many years, the strife in Guatemala was called an internal conflict. It was later upgraded to a civil war. It wasn't until the peace accords were signed in 1996 that United Nations investigators declared it a genocide. For thirty-six years, a government systematically sought to annihilate Mayan people, and the world didn't really know, didn't really see, perhaps didn't want to see. The stories of the two hundred thousand Guatemalans who died have helped to reveal the truth.

The staff at the FAFG believes that there is no possibility for healing until the ghosts have had their say. As often as possible, their work involves matching the found remains with lists of missing people. When there is a match based on location, age, sex, and eye-witness reports, the FAFG attempts to return the body to the surviving family members so that it can be buried in accordance with community tradition.

Healing requires truth-telling. Just like my desire to read Dave's autopsy report, there's a longing to know what happened and to try to understand the experience of the one who was lost. The specifics of the story matter.

Far from Guatemala, I now live in Minneapolis, a few miles from where George Floyd was killed by then-police officer Derek Chauvin. The world rose up in outrage at the story of a white police officer kneeling on the neck of another human for eight minutes and forty-six seconds. Reacting against the dehumanizing indignity of racism and brutality, the chant "Say his name!" rang through the streets of my neighborhood. People all over the world began to lift their voices, yelling in call-and-response style: "Say his name! George Floyd. Say his name! George Floyd."

One man. One death. George Floyd's story sparked a global uprising against systematic injustice. His name, his death, is the story we now tell when we are trying to explain the urgent need for upending and reconstructing broken systems.

The dead must be named, and their stories must be told.

Logistically, it would be easy for me to sweep this part of my life under a rug. It would be easy to flash my smile and pepper my social media with travel photos and videos of silly, beautiful children. It would be easy to pack the memories of my broken, dying loved ones into a box and shove it into the corner of my soul.

But I can't do that. Not to them. And not to myself.

The first time I visited the FAFG, I found it shocking to be in such close proximity to human remains. I was allowed to get up close and look carefully at the bones. I examined the pelvis of a woman who was about thirty years old. It took my breath away to be that close to a body. It was sacred. I felt like I should whisper.

After time in the laboratory, visitors walk through more cluttered hallways to a small internal patio where they can sit with a guide to ask questions. On my first visit, I asked how many cases were in their backlog. How many bodies did they have left to reconstruct? The guide almost laughed at me. She said that every hallway in the building is lined floor to ceiling with boxes. And each of those boxes contains the fragments of a human body. She said that they have entire rooms in the building stacked floor to ceiling with boxes of human remains. Thousands.

All those bodies.

All those stories.

The dead must be named, and their stories must be told. That is the only possible path to healing.

What will happen if we don't find the courage to tell their stories? What are the costs to the collective psyche when a generation does not name and revere the stories of its dead? What unravels if more Black men are killed by police, without their names being known? What is lost if those boxes of holy human remnants languish in crowded hallways for another thirty-six years?

What will happen to my heart if I skip over the story of my brother and how he died? What will happen if too much time passes between moments in which his name comes to my lips.

All those ghosts long to be named.

And it seems that haunting is within their right for those of us who refuse to learn and see and listen.

take a moment. . . .

Say the names of your lost ones. Tell their stories. Speak their truths. Post their photos.

Keep their stories fresh and tended.

Let the lost know that they hold a place within you. Don't banish them to the shadowy storage room of your mind. Let them be part of you.

If you do not, you risk an internal fragmentation, a splitting within yourself. If you don't actively remember them and the life that you shared with them, the part of you that knew and loved them languishes and dies.

On the surface it may seem easier to let go, forget, close the book, lock the door; but it is not. We are not meant to be divided, to leave pieces of our hearts lying about. We are meant to expand our capacity—to grow our memory, to create space in our hearts to hold all those that we've loved. Past and present, living and dead.

You may create moments that are uncomfortable for others when you speak of the dead. The air may leave the room for a moment as they freeze with fear and awkwardness. Their emotional uncertainty is not your work.

Say their names. Often.

Heaven

Potluck in the Sky?

I GREW UP believing in heaven. Or at least I heard a lot about heaven, and I talked a lot about heaven. For the first twenty-three years of my life, I was quite concerned with who was going and who was not, and I made it my business to try to bring more people into the first category—those who RSVP'd "Yes!" to the heaven party.

As a young evangelical, I imagined heaven as a continuous, debauchery-free, twenty-four-hour party. I pictured it with the decor of Marie Antoinette's era at Versailles: lots of pearls, velvet curtains, wigs, ornate furnishings, formal dancing, and delicious punch served with jeweled ladles.

I didn't come up with this image all by myself. I grew up with a theology that rallied around the golden streets, pearly gates, and customized mansions that await the faithful followers as a decadent reward for a life of Christian service. All this fabulousness had the added advantage of erasing the sadness from death. If your departed loved one was a Christian, there were no good-byes, just see-you-laters. We sang about heaven as a family reunion in the sky.

Death was redeemed by God. Believers would join God in an eternal union. Death wouldn't get the final word. A common refrain: there's no victory in the grave. Death was only sad if someone wasn't a Christian and therefore wouldn't be attending the eternal festivities. Those outside the flock would go to hell, which was, in my upbringing, a literal place of eternal torture.

Any early-life conversation about death or the nature of grief became co-opted into a conversation about heaven. If you can get your loved ones to convert, you can bypass the grief process because, of course, you'll just see them later at the party. If you can't get them to convert, they spend eternity in torture, which is very sad and also somewhat shameful. Perhaps it was a failure of your ability to "shine your light" that contributed to their eternal undoing.

In retrospect, I was not well equipped for the emotional nuances I now find myself swimming in. There wasn't any meaningful conversation about grief in my early years. There was pressure to live in a compellingly Christian way, and there was shame and fear about failing in that mission. But no meaningful conversation about grief.

I had no idea about death then.

But now I know unequivocally that you do have to say good-bye.

The family reunion bit is a nice thought, but you don't know if you'll meet again in any recognizable form. No one *knows* about heaven. There aren't any Tripadvisor ratings.

My friend Anne also lost her brother to suicide, and heaven gives her tremendous comfort. Heaven gives my mother a lot of comfort too. And their belief is real and measured and formed by the same heart-wrenching experiences that created my grief. There is no shallowness in the way that they understand heaven. It is a mature version of it, much less focused on bedazzled accessories than my preadolescent imaginings. Heaven is a real expression of faith and a source of hope and deep comfort.

I spoke to Anne a few months after my brother died, and she started talking about how she imagined her brother's soul existed in heaven. I felt glad for her. Glad that she had that sense of him existing somewhere. She had a sense of him at peace.

I am a little envious of that feeling, because I have no spiritual intuition or deep internal sense of "knowing" about heaven.

It brings me no comfort to think of my brother and my dad hanging out in some celestial baseball field, playing a round of catch with my grandparents and maybe, Luke, my childhood dog. It is a sweet thought, but it lives in the realm of my imagination. It doesn't land in any substantive part of my mind or soul. I don't *feel it* the way that Anne does.

The truth is that heaven doesn't matter to me right now.

My father and brother have either continued on in some form or they haven't. It is an unknowable question and, either way, they are inaccessible to me. They are there and I am here. Mentalizing about what they're doing and where they are doesn't serve me at this point in the story. It is existentially unknowable and practically inconsequential.

It isn't that I've decided to believe or not believe. The conversation isn't that organized within me. The question of where they are simply hasn't engaged either my soul or my intellectual curiosity.

I met Dr. Matt House, a treasured colleague and mentor, a few months before his father, Dr. Charles House, died of leukemia. When I met Dr. Charles, the first thing he said to me after shaking my hand was, "Well, Sherry, it seems that I'll be dying soon." I was interviewing for a job at the clinic that father and son had shared for years. To say that I was interviewing to replace him is impossible, because he was irreplaceable, but I did move into his office a few months later. When we talked about grief and his father's death, Matt, who is both a spiritual and religious person, said simply, "I believe we are eternal." And it was clear that the eternal nature of his father brought him a sense of comfort. I like this. There's no dogma or constructed images of ornately decorated gates.

I believe we are eternal. It is sufficiently open and comprehensive.

I feel my dad's presence every day. I feel him in my cells: in the shape of my muscular shoulders, when I see my eyes in the mirror. I feel him when I drive my car and when I rise hours before my family to go to the gym. He is in my body. He is in my habits. He is in my every day. He is in my past, my present, and my future.

I feel my brother's presence every time I get on a bike, or walk by the lake in my neighborhood. Every time I climb a tree or watch my kids climb trees. I think about him every time I have freshly made salsa. He is in my camping trips, my walks in the woods. My outdoor, adventurous self. He is in my memory. He is part of every conversation I have about mental health or suicide. He is part of the legacy I am trying to uphold. And redeem. My past, my present, and my future.

My lack of curiosity about heaven does not translate to a physicalist interpretation of life and death. To the contrary, I relish the mystery of it. I don't presume to know how to define and label what it might mean to be eternal.

As much eternity as I can possibly fathom, as far as my brain cells can spread, my dad and my brother are in all of it. From the beginning of conceivable time to the end of conceivable time.

That is as far as I can grasp, and that is all I need to grasp.

I'm sure I'll have my reckoning with the afterlife in due time. The unfortunate thing is that when I reach a place of knowing for sure what shape eternity might take, I will likely not be able to report back on it.

take a moment . . .

Close your eyes. Shift your focus to your breath for a moment.

Invite into your mind the image of the one you've lost. Imagine their face. Hold their name in your mouth. Perhaps ask them, in your mind, *Where are you? Where are you now?*

As you breathe, feel the question. Feel your loved one in place on the other side.

Linger as long as you'd like.

What do you think about life after death? What do you *feel* about it?

How do you connect with the remnant existence of those you've lost?

Where do you most feel their presence?

Spend some time communing with them.

Fuck It—
I'm Joining the Circus

FOUR MONTHS AFTER Dave died, I had a six pack. Not the beverage kind, the abdominal kind. My dad and my brother both died the year I turned forty. It was a year of heavy things. In addition to the crash course in death, I was running my own business and caring for three intense children. Trying to show up for my husband, trying to be a friend, and trying to deal with the developmental baggage of transitioning "over the hill," and grappling with my own mortality.

I did what every reasonable middle-aged, working professional and mother of three would do in this situation. I joined the circus.

I began practicing aerial arts: sling, split panel silks, and some flying trapeze. Aerial is equal parts yoga, dance, acrobatics, and brute strength. It was a casual hobby that I started about two years before my dad died. When I moved to Minneapolis, I needed to take up an indoor sport because it turns out that I didn't love the experience of running in two-degree weather.

I ended up at an aerial yoga class. I'm a yoga teacher, and I've been doing yoga for many years, so I thought, *Hey, this is a new take on something I already love. Sounds fantastic.* I started practicing regularly, and I realized that it's a good fit for my body type and for how my brain works. I went pretty deep; I did a teacher training and a few performances.

It wasn't until my dad died that I felt like I *needed* aerial. I felt an urgency—like I needed to move and spin and lift and train in order to survive. I needed it like I needed to breathe. Some days I trained for three hours: lifting weights in the morning, training with an aerial instructor, and then maybe practicing on my own for another hour. I sprinkled my weeks with traditional yoga and running to balance out my exercise routine.

I can't express how grateful I am that aerial was in my life during the season of death and grief. In the midst of emotional heaviness, I needed something light and playful. I needed something that would take my mind off loss. I needed to literally fly around in the sky to keep myself from being fully immersed in the sad, heavy coldness of death. I could grieve and cope effectively because I had something in my life that provided a counterbalance to all the emotional weight I was carrying. The time of grief may seem like a strange time to join the circus. But it is also the perfect time. It was so much more than a hobby—it was a healing practice and hands down the most important protector of my mental health during the years of intense grief.

When I am moving as an aerialist, I am using a different set of neurological skills, different cells than I use when I'm working as a psychologist or when I'm writing or speaking. I'm using spatial reasoning. I'm focused on physics. I'm thinking about how not to fall. My body's innate proprioception is activated. It is so, so good for our brains to diversify and built new neuronal connections. Activities like dancing, which require us to memorize steps or to watch a motion and then practice that motion, build our kinesthetic intelligence, which is a part of us somewhat stunted in most of our sedentary adult lives. Movement is one of the best protections against the cognitive decline that's commonly associated with aging.

And now I've come to know that movement is one of the most powerful healing tools. We need a diversified brain if one set of circuitry within our brains gets fatigued, or the connections between the neurons start to fray, or if we are flooded with the imbalanced neurological activation commonly associated with trauma and grief. Having a lifelong hobby or even a series of different kinds of hobbies is helpful in cultivating a robust brain that is able to stay healthy and strong while also digesting the tremendous weight of loss. And play. I can't overstate the psychological necessity of play, especially when you're in the midst of grief. Aerial is the one place where I have a break from sadness. There's no emotional complexity. There are no triggers. It is a different experience, a different existence, a true pause from the tasks and challenges in grief life.

Aerial is also a deep study in the reality that nothing stays the same. When I am learning a new trick on the sling, I feel myself growing. I feel myself changing. I watch it, try it, practice it five times. Get feedback from a teacher. If it's a simple trick, in the course of ten to fifteen minutes, I've accomplished it. Woo-hoo! Get to check that off my list. That's a great little dopamine rush for a brain that is in the midst of a yearslong slog of active grief. The dopamine hits are few and far between in my land-based life, and my brain is thirsty for simple accomplishments and a feedback loop of success.

It will take me years to learn how to live through Christmas without my dad and brother. But I can learn a new trapeze trick in a weekend.

I've never been a dancer. I have very limited background in gymnastics. I'm forty-two years old and just now learning to point my toes and work on being able to do the splits. But little by little, day by day, I feel my body learning new ways to be in the world. Living in this sense of possibility is absolutely refreshing compared to the stuckness and finality of death.

As an aerialist, I'm well known for my strength. I'm able to master complicated tricks purely because I can hold my own body weight for an extended period of time. Thanks for those shoulders, Dad. In fact, I'm so strong that when I slipped off the side of a rope suspension bridge while hiking in the Dominican Republic, I caught myself on a dangling rope and held on with one hand until I could lower to safety. It was next-level grip power that kept me from getting badly hurt.

But aerial is a lesson in counterbalancing strength with flexibility. Muscles that are too tight are vulnerable to injury—they're susceptible to being pulled or torn or detached at the tendon. An over-strengthened body is a rigid one—imagine the super muscly football player who can't reach his toes. Aerial requires a stretching practice that elongates the sinews and creates a flexible softness that prevents tearing and other injuries. Of course, an overly flexible body is problematic too. Without strong muscles to stabilize the tendons, the joints can slip out of place, becoming dislocated or vulnerable to a different set of injuries caused by hyperextension or structural weakness. Strength and flexibility are both necessary components of a high-functioning body.

And finally, aerial has filled my life with interesting people. Isolation and loneliness are a debilitating part of grief. And frankly, I'm not the best conversationalist as a grieving person. At my aerial studio, I am part of a community. I am loved because I show up and am kind, and I demonstrate a deep love for the practice. We have a built-in conversation topic. They're my troupe, and the fact that my life is a shit show is completely unknown and irrelevant to them.

I get that you may not want to go out and join the circus. Perhaps you'd like to keep your feet on the ground or in the kitchen or the metal shop. It doesn't really matter. From my perspective, the best grief-helping hobbies fit these criteria:

- Absorbing. An activity that requires you to be "all in." You cannot be distracted. You cannot dwell on a problem at work or think about a problem with your kid or think about your grief. The task requires full focus. Woodworking, glassblowing, rock climbing—if

you're not paying attention, you could get seriously
hurt. The demand for your body and your mind and
your emotional life to be completely engaged helps you
heal. Maybe painting, maybe cooking, maybe hockey,
creating board games, learning piano. The key is that
your brain is on a break from grief.

- Collaborative. Elizabeth is one of my aerial teachers.
  She is a ballerina turned rock climber, turned circus
  performer, and she is also on the autism spectrum. She
  thinks in movement. She can hardly explain things to
  me in words. She always has to show me, because her
  primary language is the language of movement. And
  that is so different from me—I am immersed in the
  world of words.

  But I've been without words more often in the midst
  of grief. The sadness swells into my throat and blocks
  the sound. Elizabeth is teaching me how to think and
  feel in motion. The healing hobby doesn't need to be
  a team sport where you're playing soccer or volleyball,
  and you have a lot of comradery with other people. But
  it is very, very helpful if your hobby can help create a
  broad network of people. People who aren't living in
  the middle of the grief story with you and can therefore
  afford you the space and time to live in another part of
  your story.

- Embodying. Most of us spend a lot of our adult lives
  detached from our bodies. We live in our minds. We
  live in our to-do lists. If we're in grief, we live in the
  heaviness. Healing involves getting back into your
  body—moving the emotion around, letting it move
  through you. We can't heal sitting still. That means that
  we must relearn how to move, how to play with our
  hands and our toes and all the muscles in between.

I appreciate that it is not always easy, as a grown-up, to walk in totally green to a new activity. There is an awkward phase and a learning curve that most of us are not comfortable with. Over and over I have found people to be so gracious, and when they have something that they love, they're often very happy to teach.

In order to become an aerialist, I've had to carve out time early in the mornings before my kids get up. A few nights a week, I take classes at the end of the day, after they go to sleep. Going deep in on a hobby costs time, energy, resources, emotional reserve, relationship capital—it is very costly. But the benefits are much greater than people realize. A hobby is an investment in your long-term well-being, neurological flexibility, physical health, relationship connections, and your capacity for joy and fun. In the midst of grief, or in the midst of a demanding grown-up life, I think we're too busy *not* to create the space in our lives for these kinds of activities. We're too busy *not* to play. We're too busy *not* to be learners who are willing to explore different spheres of life and different ways of being in our bodies.

Flying around and spinning upside down might not be your jam, but there's got to be something other than sitting in front of a computer all day.

Play is the antidote to grief. Given the universal looming of grief, whether big losses like deaths or losses like failure of important plans or being laid off at work, it would be helpful for all of us to find our best way to play. Play now. You never know how seriously you'll need it.

take a moment . . .

It can be hard to get started. Here are some steps for returning to play, especially as a grieving grown-up:

STEP 1 Write down some playful activities that you're
curious about.
- What have you always wanted to try?

- What kinds of activities are your friends and family members enjoying?
- What did you love doing as a kid?

STEP 2 Prioritize what's most playful.
- Is it novel, different from your day-to-day work life?
- Does it use your body, either your gross or fine motor skills?
- Is it something you think will bring you joy?
- Does it involve a community of others?
- Is it sufficiently engaging and focusing that you'll be "all in"?

If you answered yes to all five questions, the activity made it to your short list.

STEP 3 Plan and go!
- Pick your top two to three activities to try.
- Research communities, groups, events, and places near you where you can try it.
- Based on schedule and logistics, choose one activity to try three times.
- Put it in your calendar and lock in the plans.

STEP 4 Reflect and assess for joy. Now that you've tried it three times, assess the activity based on the following criteria:
- How did your body feel during your activity?
- What kinds of thoughts came up for you during your activity?
  - Positive thoughts.
  - Negative thoughts.
- What was your mood or emotional state while you were playing?
  - Did you laugh?
  - Did you enjoy the other people involved?
  - Were you engaged and focused?

If you've gone three times and feel like it might not be right for you, return to your brainstorming list, and repeat the exploration process.

STEP 5 Dive into play.
- Based on your reflections from this exercise, perhaps you've found your play activity.
  - Block it off in the calendar for the next three months.
  - Protect the time. Move meetings, arrange sitters, and so forth.
  - Talk with your friends and family about your play. Ask for their support. Make sure people around you know that it's a priority for you.

BIG LIST OF PLAY IDEAS

Practice yoga

Pilates

Love beer or kombucha? Start home-brewing

Take a studio art class

Join the Sierra Club or another, like an REI hiking group

Learn a musical instrument

Join a gardening club or take a class at a local nursery

Join a chess club

Train for a marathon or a 5K

Take up swimming

Ballroom, salsa, or adult ballet

Sign up for a plot in a community garden

Woodwork

Surf or scuba dive

Get into tie-dyeing fabrics

Archery

Join a cover band or start a band with friends

Start paddleboarding

Find a writer's workshop to collaborate and get feedback on your work

Learn to keep bonsai trees

Join an ultimate Frisbee team

Acroyoga

Join a community theater

Take a cartooning class

Start horseback riding

Build a model rocket

Make your own candles or soap

Fencing lessons

Bodybuilding or competitive
weight lifting

Learn flower arranging

Become a puzzles master

Join a book club

Practice origami

Write fan fiction

Join Toastmasters to improve
your public speaking skills

Take a photography class with
a local adult education
program

Take an improv class

Take a magic class

Learn needlepoint or knitting

Study a new language

Rock climbing

Rebuild a classic car

Learn jujitsu

Join a soccer league

Join a softball league

Join a hockey league (ice or field)

Beekeeping

Work with rescue animals

Learn to sew

Pottery

Tabletop gaming

Comic book writing
or illustration

Join a community choir,
orchestra, or band

Learn to tile or make mosaics

Work your way through a
cookbook

I Might Be Too Messed Up to Go to Work

SOMETIMES I DON'T think I should be a psychologist anymore.

I am supposed to be well trained in how to help prevent suicide. The premise of my job is to help people who are feeling deeply lost and hopeless.

If I'm such a fancy professional, why couldn't I "save" my own brother?

Save. It is a powerful word. I wrote it in quotes because I know, intellectually, that saving is beyond me, as a professional or as a person.

But I did try.

I tried to save him. I tried to prevent him from dying. And I couldn't.

Like many of the physicians who come my way as therapy clients, I've gotten caught in the trap of believing that preventing death is the most important part of my job.

Good doctor = Live patient. Bad doctor = Dead patient.

It sounds overly simplistic but this assumption is entrenched in the most basic foundation of the medical world. Eliminate illness, prevent death. Keep people alive.

My ego wants reassurance that I'm not a failure. Can I still be proficient at my job and also part of the tragedy of Dave's death?

I'm good at this, right? I read all the books and passed all the tests. I wrote the papers and wrestled with the big questions. I've worked with more than a thousand clients over the years. But when it counted, when I really wanted to be smart and excellent and capable, my stupid PhD did nothing to help me with the one person I most desperately wanted to help.

There are moments when grief has left me so tender. Like my soul's skin is badly sunburned and an encounter with a wisp of cotton fabric leaves me shuddering in pain.

This is not a good way to show up in the professional world. There have been many moments when I seriously considered packing up and discontinuing my work. Moments when I felt too unsteady or too fragile to be useful.

But I'm not going to stop being a psychologist. I'm going to continue, not because of my egoic meanderings about my own failures or because I have something to prove or compensate for.

When all my professional confidence and cache are stripped away, when I'm less sure of my competence and less focused on being powerful and helpful, I find myself feeling very, very human. The part of me that remains is actually profoundly useful.

I've been unlearning much of what I studied in graduate school. I've let go of formal treatment plans and strict adherence to theoretical frameworks. They don't matter, not really. Not on the human level, not to the world I'm in now.

I'm learning to come to terms with uncomfortable tenderness. I'm more aware of all I don't know and all that I can't control. I have a greater capacity to empathize and more practical wisdom. I connect more with the sadness within my clients. I feel it in a way that I didn't before, especially the sadness that is held within ambitious, successful people. The driven. The doers. The "hard work leads to good outcomes" people. The savers. The achievers. People like me.

I'm not the same psychologist I used to be. I'm less formal. I sense that my clients recognize this. They realize that they're talking with someone who is a little raw and gritty and has traveled to the land of loss and struggle. We speak the same language.

I don't feel like a professional. I've simply been entrusted with a small group of souls to love and support for however long they happen to inhabit a space in my sphere. They don't need fixing or saving, and I don't presume to hold these powers. I am not their friend, but there is a kind of companionship. I set the table and host the space at the meeting of the ambitious broken hearts club.

Now that I've been through this journey with Dave, I live quite comfortably in this raw and unraveled space. I work in a different way.

I'm unafraid.

And also, I'm very afraid.

Because I know how much it hurts when it goes badly.

take a moment . . .

How has loss shaped your professional self? Has it shifted your practices or priorities? Is your ego fragile or defended or perhaps just gone?

Grief changes so many parts of us, of course you'll work differently.

Spend time reflecting on how your work feels during this season of grief. What tasks or aspects of your work are you most drawn to? How has grief helped you to be better at your work? Deeper? More insightful? What do you find intolerable in your workday? What do you avoid? Notice the moments of your workday when you feel alive and engaged and the moments that suck the life out of you. Perhaps record these highs and lows at the end of each day.

As much as possible, try to adjust your work to maximize the tasks that are life-giving. Grief is a long slog, and you need all the energy you can muster. Work can be a helpful anchor. You may need some time away from work, but you may also find tremendous meaning and value in diving into your work in the aftermath of your loss. It is completely okay to love your work right now.

Pay careful attention to those highs and lows. This reflection is important data because it helps us discern what parts of our work fit well for us and what parts are less congruent with how grief is reshaping us.

If you feel pulled away from your typical work, notice what you are being pulled toward. Something more creative? Something more human? Something less complicated? Something more joyful?

I wouldn't make any big professional shifts in the first year after grief. Too much is unsettled. Too much of your energy is absorbed by coping with the magnitude of loss. But it is a helpful time to reflect and write. Observe your instincts and intuitions.

How can you express the new insights, deeper focus, or greater tenderness without losing the parts that seem core to your professional self?

Take the gifts. Release the baggage. Go slowly.

Freud Was Right

Death, Sex, and Trauma

I HAVE BEEN surprised by some of the ways that grief has changed me. I knew my family would change. I anticipated that my friendships and my work would change. I could have guessed that my parenting would be different.

I did not foresee the beginning of a completely new relationship between my mind, my soul, and my body. I did not anticipate that my body would feel so different. I did not expect so much cellular change.

When my mom called that Friday afternoon, before she formed the words, I knew that Dave was dead.

I felt the news in my body. Before I knew it in my mind.

I walked outside onto my back porch, and a palpable shock of electricity careened through me from the back of my skull to my fingers and toes. I felt dizzy, like I was on a terrible carnival ride.

In one instant, I experienced two forceful urges.

First, the full-bodied, overpowering desire to throw myself into some act of violence. To shriek like a wild animal and hurl something, crush something, destroy something, claw something, kill something. I looked frantically around me for something to throw—a potted plant, a shoe, anything.

Then, right on the heels of that urge, I had an absolutely overwhelming impulse for sex. And to be clear—it was not an urge to be held or make love; it was a primal drive to thrust my body up against another living body in a life-force fuck kind of way.

These instinctual reactions flooded past my well-developed prefrontal cortex and overtook me in an instant. But in the absence of something to shatter or someone to fuck, I collapsed to the ground—as many traumatized people do—and shifted back into my thinking, planning brain.

I've talked to lots of people about their "phone call" moments. There's almost always a significant physiological reaction to traumatic news. Many people fall on the ground, physically collapsing in response to the way that their world has imploded. People feel like they can't breathe. Sometimes people feel nauseous, like they've been kicked in the stomach. Sometimes people vomit. Sometimes the body shuts down, and they become numb. This isn't consciously logged as a significant physiological reaction, but it is.

The ferocity of my body's response was strange to me, even though I know that bodies have big reactions to unthinkable news. It happened in a flash and with such power that I will never forget the feeling of it.

If you know your classic Freud, you'll recognize the urge for sex and the desire for violence as the two most basic drives of the psyche, the core motivations around which the internal workings of the human psyche are organized.

Eros, or libido, the hot, fierce, passionate life force—the urge to create, reproduce, have sex—or more philosophically, the urge of the individual to surpass itself, to expand.

And Thanatos, the death instinct—cold, destructive, imploding. It is the urge of the individual to decompose itself into nothingness.

Expansion and nothingness.

They are the two most basic drives in life, evolutionary holdouts in our animal brain. I felt them both right there, right then, as my world crumbled around me. As my little brother's body was being scooped into an unglorified black plastic bag, my body reverberated like it had been struck by lightning.

In that instant I heard the voice of Thanatos within me:

> *Death is coming. It is at your doorstep. It took*
> *your father. It took your brother. You have to*
> *run. Fight. Kill. Get away from this. Get away*
> *from death. Get away from the danger that is*
> *undoing you. Hurl death away with all your*
> *might. Scream in its face. Scare it with your wild,*
> *violent craziness. Make it run far away. Make it*
> *promise to leave you alone forever.*

I wanted to kill death. I wanted to fight against Dave's death with my claws and my fangs. I wanted to bring destruction and mayhem to the audacity of death.

And then there was another voice inside of me, Eros:

> *Cling to life. Find the aliveness of a body*
> *and thrust yourself inside its chest. Grasp*
> *life. Melt into life. Return to the beginning,*
> *the origin of life, and the spark of life-*
> *filled, pulsating bodies dancing together,*
> *joining their cells to make aliveness out of*
> *nothingness. Stay alive. Fuse with life.*

I wanted to exercise my most basic capacity to bring life into being. To immerse in aliveness.

In this extraordinary somatic moment of violence and lust, I felt my body change.

I had an instantaneous realization that my cells are incredibly powerful.

And my cells wanted to live. By whatever means necessary.

On that day, my body took on a new life of its own.

If you could crack me open and look inside me, you would find a deep burn mark—like the charred scar on the trunk of a tree that's been stuck by lightning. The mark of trauma. The mark of loss. The stain of a complex grief that will never be neatly organized into my mind.

And because this flashpoint experience exceeded the neatly organized framework of my brain, my body sparked to life in a new way.

I have a new awareness, a new respect that my body has her own power and drive. From that moment, for the rest of my life, I will honor my cellular body as beautiful and made for pleasure and delight. And sometimes battle.

Above all, made for fierce aliveness.

My brother's body was shattered. But mine is whole. And so fully alive that sometimes it feels like it is bursting from its container.

I didn't expect to transform in this way, but that life-affirming, trauma-sparked force came alive that day. And now I'm living less in my head. Less certain of authority and prestige and thoughts. I care much less about what I'm supposed to be feeling or doing.

I'm much more focused on being amazing at living.

At being a survivor.

The forces of Eros and Thanatos have come alive within me. They've left me a little bit wild.

And they're not going away.

One Year

THE FIRST SIX weeks are the trauma zone:

> Can't sleep
> Cry a lot
> Manage crisis
> Attend to logistics

Around month three, I began to remember how to move in the world. My unsteady fawn legs relearned to carry my weight. I remembered normal. Death was no longer the top story in my inner newsreel. It was no longer all consuming. There was space in my mind and heart for other things.

Around six months, I could speak calmly and openly about my grief. It integrated. It felt like part of me. Tender, but not overwhelming, like an injury that requires careful accommodation but doesn't run my life.

Then came the one-year mark. It hit me with the force of a semi truck. A huge gaping hole appeared overnight in what used to be a relatively well-reconstructed version of my life.

I didn't expect it. Neither did anyone else. There were no cards. No comfort measures. Just a mini explosion that must be absorbed, or swallowed down, like a fire-eater at the circus.

May 10, 2020, marked one year after Dave's death. It fell on Mother's Day.

Dan texted me to coordinate a group FaceTime with my mom. We made arrangements, and I started typing, "Did you call Dave?" I wrote the "D-i-d" before I remembered that Dan couldn't have called Dave because Dave was dead. I deleted the letters. We are a sibling group of two now.

There's a part of me that is still waiting for him to call. Or show up on his bike.

The date on the calendar seemed to trigger a complete re-realization of death. My mind buzzed with thoughts like this: *He's not coming back. I'm never going to see him again. He's not on a trip. He's gone.* In some ways it was like I was processing these realizations for the first time.

The one-year mark also opened the door on all the lasts. The last time we walked down the street together. The last order of Chinese takeout. The last time he said my name. The last time he lay on the bed with the dog. The last phone call. The last hug. It was a flood of mundane memories that became deeply significant because they cannot be repeated.

I knew academically that death anniversaries were a significant psychological event for bereaved people. Death anniversaries are a vulnerable time for addiction relapse, drops into depression, and elevated suicide risk. The date on the calendar, the cues of the season, the reminders in the external world—all of it triggers a phenomenon of re-experiencing in which the moments of the loss play over again, loud and in surround sound, in the movie theater of the mind. In some ways the memory is worse than the first time, because now you know how it ends. You know all the suffering and grief that is to follow.

It feels like you're on a horrifying merry-go-round. And you can't get off.

And then there's Christmas. And in our family, the greatest holiday, the Super Bowl.

And then birthdays.

The first Thanksgiving was particularly hard without my dad. Even into my adulthood, he was the organizer of the feast. I don't really like to cook, and I'm not gifted in the organizational orchestration of multicourse meals. I felt lost without him, even though I'd moved all over the country and had already celebrated many Thanksgivings without him at the table. I feared that I may never sit down for a competently organized Thanksgiving meal again.

The first Christmas was also horrible. My dad was an enthusiastic merrymaker. He collected singing snowmen and tiny ceramic snow village scenes. He went overboard with the lights and the tree. He videoed every moment of gift opening and was extraordinarily lenient with sugary treats. Christmas was gaudy, bright, colorful joy. I felt pressure to carry on his enthusiasm for the sake of my own young kids. But I also felt so sad and so tired. Christmas became a combo pack of self-disappointment, shame at not being better at celebrating, sadness at his absence, and piercing loneliness. The first one I was sad. The second one, I planned an island trip and effectively canceled all traditions. No one complained, but I'm not sure that a hotel Christmas buffet really struck the same chord.

The anniversaries are particularly difficult with two deaths so close together. The first year, I was pretty much a mess from the beginning of November to New Year's and again for the month of May.

I do think it will get easier as the years go on. I'm already creating new habits and rituals to replace the nothingness. I'm finding new pacing with holidays, and am packing the months with experiences that feed my heart. I'm hoping to do a solo backpacking trip each May to honor my brother, who was born and died in May, and my dad, whose birthday falls two weeks after Dave's. I'll create some new holiday practices for myself and my kids. I believe these seasons can be redeemed from the sadness.

I'm hoping that, as time moves on, the happy, beautiful memories will grow louder and stronger and fill some of the empty space.

The loss is so deep because the love was also so deep.

take a moment . . .

Be gentle with the part of you that is lingering in disbelief. The part of you that intuitively dials the phone number. The part of you that watches for the car in the parking lot.

Even if it doesn't seem necessary at this moment, take time to plan out a memorial activity for the one-year mark. Maybe that's a visit to the gravesite, or a dinner that honors your lost one's favorite things. Maybe it is a gathering with family, or a solo camping trip. Whatever you do, please take time for grief. Make a plan.

Honor the rhythms of memory and calendar by setting time apart and creating a ritual that gives you room for grief.

How Do You Hug a Shadow?

GRIEF TURNS OFF all the sensors.

"I'm right here," you say.

But I can't see you.

I can't hear you.

I can't feel you.

I'm in a fog of darkness, and you must sit and wait for me to emerge.

Or not. I understand, either way. I understand if you decide not to wait.

A year after my dad died, six months after Dave died, my husband, Rob, said, "You're sad a lot. You've been sad a long time."

"I know," I said.

And that's my only response. It is true. There's not much more to say about it.

I have the energy to love on my kids, do some work, take care of myself. But my energy for romantic love is limited.

I can't imagine how difficult it is to be married to a grieving person. It's like trying to hug a shadow.

Sometimes I feel ashamed that I am in grief. And that my family turned out to be such a shit show, an unexpected saga of mental illness and suicide and pain. I wish that Rob had a wife who wasn't sad and had married into a family that wasn't caught in a tornado of tragedy. I'm ashamed that it is so messy and that I need him so much but have so little to give.

Neither of us would have predicted this when we met on the track team as college students a million years ago. We were bright and shiny and new then.

He hasn't complained. Through all of it, he's kept our life running: paid the bills, ordered the groceries, signed the permission slips. He's done all he knew to do to keep our family well and whole. And that was his way of loving me. He made it easy for me to spend time with my dad. He covered things while I sat beside Dave in the ICU. He supported me when I wanted to bring Dave to live in our town and when my parents stayed with us for six weeks so that my dad could go to the Mayo Clinic. He's watched me spend endless hours on my yoga mat or running around the lake by our house in my efforts to take care of myself. He's shown up in every logistical way. And that has been a tremendous gift to me.

But the heart stuff is harder. Emotional complexity isn't his strength on a good day. He's a builder and a fixer with two engineering degrees and an extensive history of crafting software companies. And this sequence of events has pushed us into the emotional big leagues. Part of my heart is stuck in this grief—in a place where he can't reach me, mired in problems that he can't fix. There's a sense of him waiting for me to emerge. Waiting for me to come back.

The scary truth is, I won't come back. I won't return. I will always carry this with me.

I'm afraid that my heart will be different in ways that he doesn't recognize and doesn't like.

I'll never again be that sweet twenty-year-old who adored him purely and completely. It was easy for him to help me and comfort me at the beginning of our life together. That girl is mostly gone and has been replaced by a fortysomething with scars, a bad attitude, and occasional nightmares. I'm fierce and strong and raw and brave, but these are not the characteristics that drew him to love me in the first place.

I'm in metamorphosis.

I won't always be sad. I'm not always sad, even now. But I know that I can never return to being the person I was before all this undid me. Some of it is the unraveling caused by middle life. We all change and grow and face some sort of reconstruction as we go through our adulthood. But my tearing down and reconstruction has been amplified by grief.

The other very difficult truth is that I like the changes. I have more clarity. My joy is deeper. My heart is wider and grittier and so very strong. I feel the beginnings of wisdom taking root within me. I like my renewed commitment to fully experiencing my life. I respect myself and have a deeper appreciation for the preciousness of those around me. In many ways, I love better.

I would never choose this sequence of events. But I won't run from what it has done to me.

I hope he won't either.

My deepest wish is that we fall in love with each other again. That the changed, matured, middle-aged versions of us will love each other as the college kids did. That we'll continue in our lives, loving each other through a series of ups and downs, of comings and goings, always finding ways to cherish the old parts that we know well and the new parts that grow out of the joys and the tragedies that befall us.

take a moment . . .

Major losses often bring about the unraveling of an attached relationship.

The disorientation caused by grief creates a million tiny cracks and strains. It is helpful to consider where the relationship is absorbing the strain. Don't come to any conclusions—just notice, just feel.

What is different? Where are you tender toward your partner? Where are you detached? What feels cooled between you?

Are there unspoken longings? Do you notice any twinges of resentment? What is difficult to speak aloud to your partner?

People grieve differently. That can breed loneliness. Without judgment or blame, have an open discussion about how the two of you approach grief in different ways: one is stoic, one is expressive; one is chaotic and disorganized, one seeks control and makes spreadsheets; one feels stuck in the past, one is eager to skip ahead to the future; one wants to talk about the person that was lost, one can hardly form the name in their mouth. Notice and name the differences.

It is also helpful to name the ways that you share grief. Perhaps you both wish to be held more. Perhaps you both long for more quiet. Perhaps you both want to put your energy toward something alive and something positive. Give language to what is transpiring between you: find the differences and the shared longings.

A season of grief is a great time to sit down for a few sessions with a relationship therapist. It may save you from a shattering amount of strain. Rob and I didn't start couples therapy until about a year after Dave died. I'm very glad that we did, and I wish that we'd done it sooner.

Parenting 101

You Must Get Out of Bed

I DON'T GET migraines.

I'm so grateful for that. They sound miserable. I've listened to friends describe nausea and sensitivity to light, an intense pain that overrides the ability to focus on anything. I know people who just have to go to bed for the afternoon, or for three days—whatever it takes to let it pass.

It sounds like there's a lot of overlap between migraines and what it feels like to parent in grief.

Here and there, throughout these years, I've stayed in bed in the dark.

Here and there, throughout these years, I've yelled or been critical or dismissive to my children because my heart was raw, and I couldn't find the clarity to keep my mouth shut.

I've missed music performances and homework sessions.

I frequently need to remove myself from the kids. Because the dead and the living should not intermingle, and some moments I feel more dead than alive. I'm living in a reality that I want to protect them from. So I pump myself up with playful, maternal kindness and ride that as long as I can until I melt and need to retreat to my bed or my office or some conference somewhere.

Grief has taken a toll on me as a mother.

There are moments when I want to look at them and say, "People I love have died. Stop complaining about your iPad battery. Stop asking for dessert. Leave me alone."

I'm afraid that these years of death and grieving will shape their childhoods. That they will enter adulthood thinking that they had a sad mother, one with a short temper, one who seemed to always be battling some invisible dragon.

That isn't what I want for them.

My children are smart and observant. They see it all. And they're not shy about expressing their disappointment in my poor parental performance. The time I was on a call with my brother's doctor and ran late to my daughter's play. I missed her part of the performance, but I didn't have the heart to tell her, so I pretended that I'd just been sitting in the back and heartily congratulated her theatrical mastery. I'm pretty sure she knew.

I want to tell them that they'll understand when they're older. When I explain all the things that were going on, they'll say, "Damn. That was a lot to deal with, Mom. I get why you were sort of a mess."

A retrospective exoneration of me won't really help them. It might help me feel better, but it won't help them in their journey to becoming who they're intended to be.

One of my kids has spent years of his childhood anxious about me dying.

He worries I'll contract a deadly case of COVID-19. Or cancer.

He says "Be careful" every time I leave the house.

He calls me when my errands take longer than he expects.

He lives in fear that his mother will die. It is such a big, scary thought for a sweet young one.

We talk through the science and the statistics. We talk about risk factors and protective factors and the fact that his momma is super fit and has a great immune system and a relentless personality.

We have similar conversations about car accidents, plane crashes, kidnappings, terrorist attacks, and other lethal threats that might befall one's mother. Talking through each one with measured consideration.

But his worry doesn't live in his head.

It lives in his heart.

His worry lives in a heart that has known loss. A heart that lost his uncle and his grandpa, two grown-ups who were playful and strong and seemed healthy.

Until they weren't. Until they were gone.

From his vantage point, death is very real. It is very possible in our family and very possible for the people he loves.

Many details of our lives still live in the shadow of grief.

My kiddo is generally happy. I am generally happy. We aren't depressed or forlorn. But there is such tenderness to the residual imprint of grief. It's just barely under the surface.

Loss forms and shifts the inner spaces of our lives.

I am working on showing up, on parenting through the migraine. We cuddle up nice and close—so their little hearts can feel the strength and warmth of my arms and my heart and my breath. Cuddles I can do, even from the cave of grief.

And that will be its own imprint.

That's all I have to offer them in a world that they know to be vulnerable to death and loss and grief.

Evidence of aliveness. And a determination to get out of bed every day.

take a moment. . . .

Maybe it is a strange question, but are you getting enough hugs? Whether or not you're parenting, physical touch is an important source of comfort and a visceral reminder of your own aliveness.

When you're swirling in grief thoughts or feeling afraid that you're not connecting well to your loved ones, touch is a powerful way to reground yourself. When your body feels the heartbeat of another body, it realigns in synchronization. Touch calms the nervous system.

If you are parenting, and the days are long and painful, scoop that kid into your arms for naps and cuddles and TV watching. Be in live bodies together.

Also consider getting a long, nourishing massage, preferably with a therapist who is trauma-sensitive or has strong insight into the mind-body connection. Tell them that you are in grief. Let the massage work through those overused muscles, the muscles that are tight and worn from containing all the grief that you carry.

Let the strength be released for a time. Practice softness. Let yourself need touch.

Friends Whose
Parents Are Alive

MY GIRLFRIENDS AND I occasionally vent about our parents. We sit by the fire with wine and popcorn and marvel at how frustrating and confusing it can be to be in adult relationships with the humans who raised us. We're all in our forties with parents in their sixties and seventies. And although we've spent our entire lives under the umbrella of parental love, this phase of life is proving to be deeply exasperating.

Gifts are a common thread of conversation. My girlfriends and I collectively have mothers who select odd and unpredictable gifts: a picture book featuring horses and inspirational quotes, a pair of antique opera glasses with no apparent use or meaning. My mom sent me a box of painted rocks for my fortieth birthday. Literally, a box of rocks.

Our parent banter is mostly loving and funny. We gently one-up each other with stories of bizarre and quirky parental interactions. We laugh hard and occasionally roll our eyes.

Sometimes we venture into actually complaining about our parents. Complaining about their shortcomings, complexities, and idiosyncrasies. Our fireside conversations are a place to vent our pain.

My dad was an imperfect parent. And it was important that, as his daughter, I made the space and time to heal from the ways he hurt me or failed to see what I needed or love me for who I was. I, like all people, have had to unpack some of the baggage of my childhood.

I spent a chunk of my twenties feeling critical of my dad. I imagined all the ways he could have been a better father to me. I spent time mentally tracking all the things that I wished he would have talked about with me. I noted all the ways that he failed to see and understand me. I meandered through anger and sadness, disappointment, some judgment, and some entitlement.

That's the reality of parents and kids. There were lots of ways that we missed each other. Lots of ways I was left hurt, sad, and sometimes lonely.

But I have to be honest: all that has subsided now. I'm not really into venting these days. I don't wish to complain about his shortcomings or remember the hurts of the past.

I would take my emotionally stunted, noncommunicative, neurotic dad back any day.

Recently the dinner conversation with my girlfriends ventured solidly into complaining. One friend was frustrated and seemed to be mocking her dad's latest emotional blunder. I empathized with my friend, but I also found myself getting a bit defensive and almost aligning with her father. I had to take a longer-than-normal trip to the restroom to get my judgment in check.

The thing that I didn't say: *I don't want to hear about how annoying your dad is. STFU! At least you have a dad. My dad is* dead.

Of course, I didn't say this. I'm sure she'll have her own future moments of missing her father, and perhaps her own missing will be accompanied by a similar surrender of grievances. That is her journey to traverse.

Relationships between parents and children are complex. They shift and change as we navigate the stages of our lives. It is impossible to fully anticipate what will be healed and what will be broken when our parents are no longer here to be the source of our frustration or the plot of a benign story shared with friends over drinks.

I'm much gentler with my dad now that he's gone. My memory is skewed toward the positive. I've forgotten most of the stories anchored in frustration and disappointment.

I simply miss him.

And I am so very grateful for all that he was to me.

take a moment . . .

Therapists love giving letter-writing assignments. This book wouldn't be complete without one.

Write a letter to the one you lost. Organize it into four sections.

1 What you miss about them.
2 The grievances that you choose to let go of. Forgiveness that you offer.
3 The mistakes that you wish to be released from. Forgiveness you request.
4 Your gratitude. Acknowledge the gifts that they left with you.

Write this letter as a form of conversation with the lost one. The deep, heartfelt things that you'd like to say.

Find a quiet, sacred space. Maybe their gravesite or favorite tree or a canoe in the middle of the lake.

Read it aloud to them.

Public Nudity

MY FRIEND KIM lost her husband to suicide eighteen years ago. His name was Woody, and he was a startup founder who stumbled into some sleep problems and ended up with an SSRI prescription from his general practitioner. With virtually no risk factors, he ended his life in what seemed like a medication-related fog of agitated depression.

As the years have gone by, Kim has become an expert on the suicide risks of medications. She's on FDA advisory boards and regularly testifies before federal committees. She helps raise awareness about the dangers of inappropriate prescribing and has been part of the team that has pushed for black-box labels to warn of the suicide risks associated with some psychiatric medications.

Kim's life was redirected by her husband's loss. Of course, the tremendous loss disrupted her. But over the years, advocacy has become a core part of her life. She's become powerful, strong, wise, and a champion for thousands of other people.

Richard Tedeschi and Lawrence Calhoun, from the University of North Carolina at Charlotte, have spent the last twenty years researching a concept called posttraumatic growth.[1] It is the idea that—for some people—a traumatic experience amplifies personal growth. You emerge from the terrible event as a better person than you were before, more connected to your sense of meaning and your ability to make positive contributions to the world. Nelson Mandela, Maya Angelou, Viktor Frankl are people who lived through horrendous things and used the power of their experience to positively reshape the world around them.

People love the idea of posttraumatic growth. But if you're casual with it, it can be morphed into *everything happens for a reason*. I loathe when people say this. I deeply mistrust the motivations and worldview behind this statement. The words seem to imply that everyone will come out better on the other side of their pain, if they do the right things. And while that is true for some, many people do not come out better on the other side—they come out with survival scars and an empty spot in their hearts.

I dislike the *everything happens for a reason* comment because it is often said as a thinly veiled attempt to put a nice bow on the bleeding stub of an amputation. It is a lazy acknowledgment of suffering and a rush to apply a thin salve of comfort. To the person who hears these words, they are an unhelpful pressure to rush past sorrow and pain and begin a quest for reason reconnaissance.

This is happening for a reason is often offered alongside the cousin sentiment of *God doesn't give someone more than they can handle*. Blah. As if God is up in the heaven lands with some kind of rating system, doling out hardship based on an arbitrary metric of spiritual strength. I certainly hope not.

Well-meaning people have been saying versions of this to me all my life, mostly related to my mom's experience with multiple sclerosis. MS is a difficult disease because it is so unpredictable. When I was about fifteen, my mom's symptoms were worsening, my dad was out of work—things were very, very hard at my house. Some well-meaning church friend told me that my mom was one of the strongest among us, that is why God was allowing her to carry more than her fair share of hardship. With no small tinge of teenage sass, I said: "Nope. Her choices are fall apart or keep going. She's choosing to keep going. That is all. God doesn't have much to do with it."

Even as a child, I rebelled against the pressure applied by well-meaning adults to identify and embrace a silver lining. I did not wish to participate.

Some things are just broken. Let them be broken.

I wish people had simply said, "You are loved just as you are. You probably won't feel like this forever, but it is okay to feel it now."

Things don't happen *for a reason*, but it is possible to *make meaning* out of brokenness. It is nuanced.

Posttraumatic growth implies that you have reshaped your life in beautiful ways. It is deep soul work combined with the right opportunities for expression. Growth is not a process of logic or reason or rationality or finding a missing piece to complete a puzzle.

It happens from the inside.

Ten months to the day after Dave died, I was testifying before the Minnesota legislature about the lack of safety within sober houses. I was asking them to support legislation that would provide more accountability.

This was my attempt to take a page from Kim's playbook and tell Dave's story to people who may be able to influence positive change.

Testifying before a room full of busy, distracted politicians is a little bit like standing naked before a group of senior citizens deeply involved in a night of bingo. They see that you're there, they notice the oddity of your vulnerability, they don't mock you, and they aren't unkind, but, truth be told, they'd rather return to their game. "Someone get that girl a robe so we can get on with it."

After three rounds of testimony to different legislative bodies, I stood before a senate budget committee. It was different this time. As I spoke, the chair of the committee started to wipe tears from his face. He removed his glasses. He looked away.

He rested his forehead in the palm of his hand. And then he said this: "We've got a gap here in our system . . . I just have to say. I'm grieved and I'm angry . . . And I'll tell you, I'm committed to something coming out of this. I don't want any more sisters to show up here." He put his forehead back in his hand and rested his head there for a moment.

I cried so many tears in response to this. It was so meaningful that he acknowledged that the mental health system had a bit of responsibility for what happened to Dave. It wasn't mine alone to carry. It was healing to see his compassion toward Dave and toward me. It was gratifying to speak Dave's name in the hearing and to let these leaders know that my brother used to be here and now he isn't anymore. It was important to ask them to pay more attention to the vulnerable places in the mental health care system.

Advocating for this legislation wasn't an attempt to make good come from Dave's death. Nothing will ever redeem his loss for me. But it was an attempt to honor him.

And it was a "good" thing to do.

But it didn't really make my soul sing. It was very, very draining.

I wonder if posttraumatic growth should feel more "growthy."

What is clear to me is that grief won't be rushed into some kind of agenda. You can't impose reason or meaning on it. You can't take actions to alleviate the pain.

Growth, if it comes, comes in its own time and from the inside out.

Too Strong for
My Own Good

STRENGTH CAN BE a problem.

During the dying years, I felt myself becoming too strong. Too used to pain.

Death has changed the landscape of me so much so that there were moments when I was no longer clear about what to hold on to and what to let go of.

I remember thinking: *This cancer is going to kill him. Prepare yourself. Brace yourself. Hold on for the wild ride. Be prepared for the hard things.*

I remember thinking: *He is going to die this week. Breathe. Hold it together. Stay calm.*

I remember thinking: *He will not make it. You have to let him go. Let him go!*

I remember thinking: *No one is coming to save you. No one is coming to help. You have only yourself. Hold it together.*

All these thoughts and a thousand more like them amassed during the dying years. Slowly, the heart calluses set in. I hardened. I swallowed my tears. I grew stronger. I faced all the decisions and moments with my eyes wide open and my brain in focus. I didn't collapse. I wiped up the blood. I talked to the doctors. I read the autopsy report. I showed up as the well-resourced, competent caregiver that I'd been raised to be.

But it is possible that I went too far.

My inner voice became stern and pressing. Like a rigid Olympic coach urging higher and higher levels of performance. Training. Discipline. Mental toughness. Grit. Stick-to-itiveness.

I'm a high performer. I get things done. I follow through on the outcomes that I set for myself. A fighter, like my dad.

This approach helped me manage the challenges of supporting my dad and brother while they were sick and dying, but it didn't help me in grief. It was useless after they died.

My psychologist mind knows that I experienced a shift in worldview. I developed a new set of assumptions based on the losses around me. I began to see everything through a filter of loss. I no longer believed that the people I love will reliably be alive next year, or maybe even tomorrow. Somewhere in the recesses of my heart, I started preparing for everyone to die. My children. My husband. My mother. My friends. It wasn't conscious; it just happened in subtle detachment.

A new assumption: everything is fleeting, and everyone can die.

I willed myself to get comfortable with that feeling. To face it with a forced courage. To muscle myself through the existential awareness of the universality of death and the fragility of life.

My heartbreak masqueraded as strength.

In retrospect, *let them go* was a harsh and compassionless thing for me to say to myself. It didn't honor my love for them, or my tenderness. It was an action item, but it didn't give me much time to breathe. It was spoken as a command.

I tried to protect the tenderness of my heart by doing what I thought I was supposed to do. I told myself I was *fine* and would be *fine* no matter what befell me.

Because of this determined "strength," it is possible that I began to release myself from love, from marriage, from parenting, from friendship. I prepared so well, got so comfortable with endings, that I stopped hugging others long and tight.

Some people think that the deep recognition of impermanence is enlightenment. Nonattachment is the aspiration of Buddhists and Stoics.

The existentialist asserts that one must face the certainty of nonbeing before one can fully realize freedom and responsibility.

For me, the way I began to go about letting go was not enlightenment but foreclosure. Or perhaps spiritual bypassing. To face tragedy and loss with an internal scolding of *you're fine* was a denial of my own nature.

I missed a key piece.

About a year after Dave died, I had the opportunity to participate in a course of MDMA-assisted psychotherapy. This is a newish treatment and, as of this writing, it is in the final stages of FDA approval for treating posttraumatic stress disorder. In this model, a patient uses a dose of MDMA during talk therapy. MDMA (Methylenedioxymethamphetamine) is commonly known in nonmedical circles as the drug ecstasy. It is incredibly effective in helping people process trauma because it reduces the activity of the fear center of the brain, the amygdala, and increases a subjective sense of empathy. It allows the patient to engage with their trauma experience with softness and compassion rather than fear.

During my first session, I returned to the memory of my dad's death. In my mind, I saw the event as a neutral, third-party observer, not through my own eyes as it had unfolded in my "real" experience. In the session, I hovered over our family as we gathered around the deathbed. From that vantage point, I saw myself sitting there, holding my dad's hand, trying so hard to love him well. When this happened in "real" life, I was completely focused on my dad's experience: keeping him comfortable, sending him off well. Immediately after he died, my focus shifted to my mom and brothers. Within twenty-four hours I was home and parenting and managing Dave's crisis.

However, in the treatment session, I saw myself differently at the moment of my dad's death. I saw all my vulnerability and sadness. I saw a daughter losing her daddy. I saw how young I was and how scared I was. As I observed this scene, I broke open with immense compassion for that young woman and the little girl living inside of her. I wanted to scoop her up and rock her and kiss her forehead and let her tears soak into my skin.

I had such deep, tender love for her.

For me.

In that moment, I began to feel a different strength. Not grit or endurance or toughness.

The strength of love.

I *thought* that love had been my strength before. But it wasn't. Not really. Not completely.

My love was oriented toward everyone else: my family, my clients. It didn't start with me; it wasn't *for* me. I saw myself as the tool to accomplish hard things, not as a vessel filled with love, with enough internal supply to overflow onto those around me.

I was stern and harsh to myself, and that helped me to believe that I was strong. Grief is teaching me how to source love and tenderness from that which I hold for myself. The love that I hold simply because I am here. And I am a beloved creature.

It is a different strength. Not a push or a pull. Not a letting go or a clinging tightly. It is a gentle holding. It is presence.

It is love.

take a moment....

Find a piece of paper and draw a line down the center to create two columns. At the top of one column, write "Hold On"; on the other, write "Let Go." Make a list (and it might be really long) of the parts of the dying and grieving that you wish to release and the parts of the dying and grieving that you wish to integrate permanently within yourself.

I'll go first with a few examples.

HOLD ON	LET GO
Every memory of my dad playing with my kids	Any residual beliefs that I could have prevented Dave's death
The kindnesses of those who acknowledged my losses	Fear that others I love will die
My new understanding of love for myself	Any anger I hold toward Dave

Wait, How Many Kids
Do You Have?

SPEAKING OF TRANSFORMATION.

A little girl joined our family in the middle of all this death and grief. She was seven when she came to us. Her biological parents loved her, but they got lost in addiction and could no longer care for her.

Reorganizing our family has not been easy for any of us. But she has shown up with joy and tenacity and an openhearted eagerness to begin again.

When I feel sad and lost in my own grief, I watch her.

As a young child, she had to say good-bye to her mom and her dad and her brother and move across the country to begin life with strangers. The loss she's experienced is unimaginable to most of us.

She is my teacher in how to have a resilient heart. She knows, better than anyone else I know, how to steady herself against sadness and instead decide to go outside and play, or draw, or read a book.

She came to live with us nine months after my dad's cancer diagnosis and after Dave's first narrow escape at the hospital in Montana. She came to us just as the shadow of death had begun to cast its shade over our family.

I've been in grief the entire time I've been a momma to her. She's known me only as someone who carries a heaviness, who is prone to tears, who often seems tired. And I've known her only as someone who is fighting for a place in the world, who is seeking love and belonging from a world that has not always been kind to her.

We're both battling the demons of loss.

Grief has cracked me open. And this is the best outcome: there is more space inside of me.

I felt open enough to say yes to a drastic, messy dismantling and rebuilding of our nuclear family. The addition of a child, a new beginning for my war-worn heart and for hers. I'm not sure I would've had the strength for so much disruption if I hadn't been so deeply aware of the shadow of death. When I was asked to take her, I was already living in a world that was falling apart around me. I was already living in disruption, but I was beginning to find my bearings.

My heart was open to being rearranged.

It has not been easy to add a child midway through our family story. It was never our plan. Our lives were complicated already. There have been many moments when I've made a mess of it.

But she is at the heart of all that is beautiful in this story: An expansion of love that is bigger and stronger than the emptiness of grief. A messy, bighearted courage that is willing to take a risk despite being deeply acquainted with the pain of loss.

A determination to turn toward the fullness of life.

Sneaky Reemergence
of Belief

A STRANGE THING has happened in the midst of all of this grief. I've starting seeing magic.

Or maybe I've started believing in God again.

I don't really know what label to use.

But I do know that I am becoming aware that something outside of me is helping.

I was sitting in a living room in San Diego with two friends, Kelsey and Anita, and we started talking about poetry. It was a few days before the one-year mark of my dad's death. I mentioned my renewed interest in Rilke after reading about his muse Lou Andreas-Salomé. Anita asked me if I'd read Rilke's collection of eulogies.

I hadn't. She described how beautiful they were and what they meant to her.

I asked her if she would read one aloud.

This felt like an unusual question, but Anita didn't hesitate.

And the three of us sat with tears streaming down our faces while she read the first half of the first eulogy.

The words sank straight into me. I interrupted her to ask her to read these lines twice:

> *Fling the emptiness out of your arms*
> *Into the spaces we breathe; perhaps the birds*
> *Will feel the expanded air with more*
> *   passionate flying*[1]

I bought the book a few hours later. The first eulogy became my meditation on the anniversary of my dad's death. The words anchored me as I joined my family in releasing his ashes into the lake in the burned down forest near my childhood home.

Fling the emptiness out of your arms. Release the ash to the water.

Into the spaces we breathe. Death is part of you, in you. You no longer have to hold it tightly or fear it. There is room for death and life within you.

The birds will feel the expanded air... Release the ashes to the larger cycle of things. To the air, to the water, to the next round of aliveness.

It was magic to me: That I would meet that person on that day, and that she would recommend the exact words that would serve as the necessary balm for my soul. The words that would narrate the sacrament of release in just the right way. The words that would bring beauty to the empty place within me.

A few days after Dave died, I found myself sobbing uncontrollably. My mind was overwhelmed with guilt and with racing thoughts. I was alone in a hotel room. I ran a warm bath, did some deep breathing.

And I called my friend Melissa.

Melissa and I spent a year occupying the same attic office during our predoctoral fellowship at Yale University School of Medicine. She's extraordinarily easy to love. She'd ascend into the office early in the morning with a gigantic iced coffee from Dunkin' Donuts. She called me Sher-Bear and used phrases like "warm fuzzies" and "cold pricklies." She'd host craft parties and was exuberantly affectionate with my toddler-aged son. And she's smart. She went on to become a professor and researcher with deep expertise in school-based mental health care.

Our year together was over a decade ago. We text occasionally, but we're not "everyday" friends.

In the past ten years, Melissa has said good-bye to her mom, and has been through a divorce and a traumatic injury to one of her children. I knew that she was the person I wanted to talk to as I sobbed in the hotel bathtub. She is a busy professional and a mom of two young kids, so the chances of getting her on the phone were slim.

But she answered. And she listened to me recount every reason I could think of to blame myself for Dave's death. It was ugly and convoluted. I was a little drunk on whiskey and way drunk on tears. The grief was so raw and unprocessed that none of it made much sense.

She was absolutely the perfect person to talk to. I don't remember anything she said. But I remember feeling understood and loved. Loved despite the mess I felt inside. Loved despite all the things that I wish I had done differently with my brother. Loved despite my imperfect ability to love.

The conversation had a little bit of magic in it.

I felt the first tiny moment of healing begin right then as I sat in a bathtub, talking to a friend from long ago. I felt a little glimmer of possibility that I would not implode.

My husband and I have both given our energy to building our lives outside of the families and communities that we came from. We're bootstrappers, growing businesses from the ground up. We've moved around a lot. We've worked and pushed to rise to a level of achievement that we are proud of, but that has also isolated us. We have deep friendships, but we've not necessarily made it a priority to be present for the ups and downs of other people's lives, especially since our people are now scattered across the world.

That's changing within me. Provision is changing me.

I want to show up. To have a poem to offer. To be available to take the phone call from the sobbing friend.

The other thing that's changing is that I now feel a deep sense of faith that I will be okay. That the person or thing that I need will present itself in the right time.

My friend Patrick Combs is a Joseph Campbell fan. He brings Campbell's work to life as he talks about magical doorways that open in the course of the hero's journey.

> *If you do follow your bliss you put yourself on*
> *a kind of track that has been there all the while,*
> *waiting for you, and the life that you ought to*
> *be living is the one you are living. When you*
> *can see that, you begin to meet people who are*
> *in your field of bliss, and they open doors to*
> *you. I say, follow your bliss and don't be afraid,*
> *and doors will open where you didn't know*
> *they were going to be.*[2]

I heard Patrick give a talk about this quote about four months after Dave died. I was in Italy as an invited helper for a retreat that Patrick was leading with his business partner, and our mutual friend, Eric. To my ears, these words sounded whimsical and ethereal and not very grounded in reality. They felt good, but weren't graspable in the moment.

However, something happened as I chewed on these words in my mind. I *wanted* them to be true. I wanted the pursuit of deep joy to be the core ingredient in the recipe for a good life. Campbell says "bliss," but I like the word *joy* better. I want joy to be the key to the doors opening.

I wanted that kind of joy for Dave. I wanted him to encounter open doors borne out of his heart coming alive. I wish that he could have felt that the world was available and open to him—not that he was surrounded by insurmountable stone walls. I wish that he'd found a healthy group of mentors and other joy seekers who could've helped open doors for him.

I also wanted those words to be true for me. I wanted there to be some driver beyond the *work* of caring for people and the work of building a career and successful life. I wanted permission to not have to be so strong or so sad. Alongside all this grief and death, I wanted permission to double down on joy.

I don't mean hedonistic pleasure; I mean joy. This kind of joy requires a release of control, a loosening of the fiercely strong grip. It requires trust. It requires faith that it is safe to live with an open heart despite the presence of grief and the certainty of loss. Perhaps a faith that someone or something is watching out, protecting the fragile shoots of joy as they grow from the mud of grief.

I have a complex relationship with faith. It is clear that many parts of my evangelical upbringing no longer fit. But a large part of my inner world dwells in mystery and a deep assurance that some force is here. Is watching. Is helping.

Patrick's language (via Joseph Campbell) is not the language of religion. It is the language of story, of magic. But I have found it to be helpful in reopening my pursuit of joy and my deep sense of provision, of the divine presence of help. It has given me an ability to relax into an assurance that I don't have to solve all the problems or manage all the contingencies. My job is to show up with an open heart, with love, and with intention, and perhaps with a little circus fun.

We're All Grieving

I SEE GRIEF everywhere now.

Last week I helped an entrepreneur organize a memorial event for his business. He's shutting it down. We're gathering the employees for a photo slideshow and an exchange of stories and memories. This practice is intended to help everyone say good-bye and to name the heaviness of loss.

A little subset of my clinical practice consists of women physicians, specifically surgeons and emergency doctors. Our work together includes lots of topics: parenting, the ups and downs of marriage, sexism, family-of-origin stuff. But mostly it is grief work. Grief over the moments when they weren't able to help their patients. Grief about the impossible problems they face every day. Grief at not having more time, ability, energy, wisdom, patience. Grief about lost parents and distanced kids.

There's a deep vulnerability to grief among those who live full lives. Those who pour themselves into creating businesses and meaningful vocations, those who form deep relationships and open themselves to connection with others. The more touch-points you have with the world around you, the higher the likelihood that you will encounter grief. The more you hope for, the more you stand to lose.

The deeper your love and openheartedness, the more openings for pain to land. Like light and shadow, fullness and loss are inextricably connected.

Grief is a marker of a beautiful, full life.

As I honor the griefs that have entered my life, I've begun to see my work as a kind of subversive grief boot camp. Without saying it out loud, I'm trying to help the movers and shakers of the world find a sense of comfort in loss. To prepare for the certainty of grief with open eyes and an emotional courage that accepts grief as the trade-off for love and ambition. What if all of us began to embrace grief? What if we stopped treating grief as a weakness to hide or relegate to the margins of a full life, but instead welcomed it as a teacher? As a companion?

For most of us, death is an edge state. It is not a commonly occurring part of life. We'll have intimate experience with death a handful of times during our lives.

But grief is not limited to stories involving death.

Grief is at the center. Loss weaves in and out of our lives all the time, every day, in big and small ways. In our aging bodies, in our work, in our relationships, in all our attempts, in our experience of the world around us. It is unavoidable and universal. The more we fear and avoid the feeling of it, the more angst we create for ourselves.

Let's get comfortable here in the land of grief.

We live here. We might as well settle in.

I'm Okay

I KNOW THIS book is sad.

The truth is that I am sad. And if you've spent the time to read it, I'm guessing you're sad too.

I have watched my own grief with both reverence and horror. It grows and recedes and follows its own whims.

I suppose it is like living with a caged wolf that no one else can see. In some moments, it is gnarling and growling, lashing out from its anger and pain. And then it gets tired and plops down for a nap. It is largely wild and untamable, but it has good instincts, and it is regal and ruggedly beautiful. It never goes away. And it never destroys me. But it is always there.

When people ask me how I am, I usually respond, "I'm okay." I don't say it like a mumbling teen. I say it with assurance and pride, like someone who just fell off their skateboard and flashes a thumbs-up while yelling to the concerned onlookers: "I'm okay!"

I am used to the wolf now. And it is used to me. That doesn't mean it's tame. But we've found some strategies for peaceful coexistence.

And that feels right.

Loss changed me. And grief is now my companion.

And I'm okay.

Afterword

MOST OF THESE words were written within a year of Dave's death. This book recorded my inner experiences in real time, mostly on airplanes and in the very early hours of the morning. It is a snapshot, and if it feels raw, that's because it lacks the tempering of time.

The words contained here do not constitute the final word on my grief experience, or anyone else's. I have no doubt that my thoughts and feelings will shift with time and in response to subsequent encounters with both loss and love.

As I've been working with the publisher and finalizing the manuscript, I've entered a third grief. The little girl, whom I'd hoped would be my forever daughter, left our family after 1,267 days in our home. A father, a brother, a daughter. My psychology colleagues would call this cumulative grief and caution me that griefs can easily become tangled together. Yep, it is definitely tangled.

I live here now, in the land of grief. So I'm unpacking my throw pillows and framed art.

I host a table and sit in conversation with other grieving people. Together we take moments to notice curiously how grief is changing us and what grief is teaching us. And we cry and pass the tissues and put on the teapot. And we give hugs and tell stories that make us laugh.

From my beautiful, cracked-open heart to yours, thank you for joining me in these pages.

Acknowledgments

I AM DEEPLY grateful to my mother, Marcia, my brother Dan, and my husband, Rob. The three of them lived these experiences with me. And the three of them understood and supported my need to write about our family. They each read early versions of this manuscript and helped craft what it has become. We've been brave together, and I'm so proud of us.

I've run out of ways to thank Rob for his ever-present, unconditional love. He has been a key ingredient in everything that is good in my life.

And to my sons, Fin and Fisher, who share my love of words and story. Thank you for cheering me on and understanding that the quiet Saturday mornings I spent writing on the couch were sacred and important.

To Genesis and Gage, you were both an integral part of this story. I hope that this book will help you know and understand your family and the tender love that we have for both of you.

This book has had many advocates. Nikki Van Noy, who shares the experience of losing a brother and a father, encouraged me in a way that went right to my core. She also connected me to Coleen O'Shea, who later became my agent and the persevering champion of this book. Coleen went rounds with different publishers even though "grief books don't sell." We were about to give up when Coleen got the book to Diana Ventimiglia at Sounds True. Diana read the early chapters just as she was saying good-bye to her mother. Our shared grief ignited her belief in this project, and she became its editor and midwife.

I'm still picking my jaw up off the floor in delighted shock that I get to be part of the Sounds True community.

I am deeply indebted to my friend Tyler Watson, who read the first version of this manuscript with such care that I felt myself becoming a better writer as I went line by line through his feedback.

I'm also grateful to Tucker Max and Philip McKernan, who helped to shape the structure and focus during Scribe's One Last Book memoir workshop. And I'm grateful to Berit Coleman, who wielded her masterful command of the English language with kindness and precision.

My heart has been held together by the duct tape of friendship. Carey Watson, who has been a consistent part of the rhythm of my life longer than any other friend. Thank you for holding so many of my highs and lows. I'm not sure I'd be here without Kim Witczak, Kelly Street, Kelsey Ramsden, Liz Vogt, Jamie Larson Jones, and Brooke Bergman Parr. You were my confidants, helpers, and companions during some of my darkest hours. I'm also grateful to Melissa Maras, Megan Mayberry, and Kia Asberg for their steady presence and encouragement despite time and distance.

A huge thanks is due to the aerial community in the Twin Cities, especially Hayley and Cade at Fly Freak Studio, Sherri at Flying Colors Trapeze, and the teams at Twin Cities Trapeze Center, Pneumatic Arts, and Circus Vargas. And my dear coach Lynn Lunny, who shares the experience of losing a brother to suicide. You provided healing movement, play, and easy comradery when I was desperate to grow more strength and grace.

Finally, I am deeply grateful to the many clients that I've had over the years. Your openheartedness has helped me to become more openhearted. Your trust has helped me practice trust. Your courage has grown my courage. I'm honored to spend precious moments growing alongside you.

Notes

Suicide and the Mental Gymnastics of Talking to Kids

1. Ronnie Janoff-Bulman, *Shattered Assumptions: Towards a New Psychology of Trauma* (New York: Free Press, 2002).

Disney: Death and Murder for Children

1. Kristen Anderson-Lopez, Robert Lopez, "The Next Right Thing," track 8, *Frozen II* soundtrack, Walt Disney Records, 2019.

2. Ian Colman, Mila Kingsbury, Murray Weeks, Anushka Ataullahjan, Marc-Andre Belair, Jennifer Dykxhoorn, Katie Hynes, Alexandra Loro, Michael S. Martin, Kiyuri Naicker, Nathaniel Pollock, Corneliu Rusu, James B. Kirkbride, and Sir Henry Dale, "CARTOONS KILL: Casualties in Animated Recreational Theater in an Objective Observational New Study of Kids' Introduction to Loss of Life," *BMJ* 349 (December 2014), doi:10.1136/bmj.g7184.

This Is Not What I Ordered

1. "Esophageal Cancer," Mayo Clinic, mayoclinic.org /diseases-conditions/esophageal-cancer/symptoms-causes /syc-20356084.

Yoga with Dad

1. Bessel van der Kolk, *The Body Keeps Score: Brain, Mind, and Body in the Healing of Trauma* (New York: Penguin Books, 2015).

Binge-Watching Is My Transitional Object

1. *The West Wing*, created by Alan Sorkin (Los Angeles: John Wells Productions, 1999–2006).

Dave Is Going to Die

1. Neal J. Roese, "'I Knew It All Along . . . Didn't I?'— Understanding Hindsight Bias," Association for Psychological Science, Sept. 6, 2012, psychologicalscience .org/news/releases/i-knew-it-all-along-didnt-i -understanding-hindsight-bias.html.

It Could Be Me

1. "Facts About Suicide: Suicide Is a Leading Cause of Death," Centers for Disease Control and Prevention, cdc.gov /suicide/facts/index.html.
2. US Department of Veterans Affairs, *2019 National Veteran Suicide Prevention Annual Report*, September 2019, dropbox.com/s/b1umdnwi9fsdsln/2019_National _Veteran_Suicide_Prevention_Annual_Report_508.pdf?dl=0.
3. Jameson K. Hirsch, Paul R, Duberstein, Kenneth R. Conner, Marnin J. Heisel, Anthony Beckman, Nathan Franus, and Yeates Conwell, "Future Orientation Moderates the Relationship between Functional Status and Suicide Ideation in Depressed Adults," *Depression & Anxiety* 24, no. 3 (January 2007): 196–201, DOI: 10.1002/da.20224.
4. Daniel Goldstein, "The Battle Between Your Present and Future Self," TEDSalon New York, 2011, ted.com/talks /daniel_goldstein_the_battle_between_your_present_and _future_self.

When Lifelines Become Entangled

1. J. K. Rowling, *Harry Potter and the Order of the Phoenix* (New York: Arthur A. Levine Books/2004).

Death as Light and Feathers

1. Mary Oliver, "White Owl Flies Into and Out of the Field," in *House of Light* (Boston: Beacon Press, 1990).

Public Nudity

1. Lawrence Calhoun and Richard Tedeschi, *The Handbook of Posttraumatic Growth: Research and Practice* (Abingdon-on-Thames, UK: Routledge, 2006).

Sneaky Reemergence of Belief

1. Rainer Maria Rilke, *Duino Elegies*, trans. (Berlin, Ger.: Insel-Verlag, 1923).
2. Joseph Campbell with Bill Moyers, *The Power of the Myth* (New York: Anchor, 1991).

Resources

Mental Health

National Suicide Prevention Hotline:
   1-800-273-8255
American Foundation for Suicide Prevention: afsp.org
National Alliance on Mental Illness: nami.org
Suicide Awareness Voices of Education: save.org

Cancer, Death, and Dying

American Cancer Society: cancer.org
International Association for Hospice and
   Palliative Care: hospicecare.com
The Elisabeth Kübler Ross Foundation:
   ekrfoundation.org
Open to Hope: opentohope.com
Terrible, Thanks for Asking: ttfa.org

Other Helpful Books on Grief

George A. Bonanno. *The Other Side of Sadness:
   What the New Science of Bereavement Tells
   Us About Life After Loss.* New York: Basic
   Books, 2009.
Joan Didion. *The Year of Magical Thinking.* New
   York: Albert A. Knopf, 2005.

Megan Divine. *It's OK That You're Not OK: Meeting Grief and Loss in a Culture That Doesn't Understand*. Boulder, CO: Sounds True, 2017.

Stephen and Ondrea Levine. *The Grief Process: Meditations for Healing*. Boulder, CO: Sounds True, 1994.

Nicholas Wolterstorff. *Lament for a Son*. Grand Rapids, MI: Eerdmans, 1987.

About the Author

DR. SHERRY WALLING is a clinical psychologist and mental health advocate. Her company, ZenFounder, provides mental health resources to entrepreneurs and organizations to help them successfully navigate loss, transition, burnout, and high intensity growth.

Seth Godin described her number-one bestselling first book, *The Entrepreneur's Guide to Keeping Your Shit Together* as "a personal, generous and incredibly useful guide to staying sane and changing the world at the same time."

Sherry hosts the *ZenFounder* podcast, which has been called a "must listen" by both *Forbes* and *Entrepreneur*. She speaks on loss, burnout, trauma, and resilience to audiences around the world.

Sherry has a PhD in clinical psychology and master's degrees in both psychology and theology. She is a graduate of UC Davis and Fuller Seminary School of Psychology. She completed residential research fellowships at Yale University School of Medicine and the National Center for PTSD affiliated with Boston University School of Medicine. Her academic work in trauma and burnout has been published in numerous peer-reviewed journals such as the *Journal of Traumatic Stress*.

Sherry will always be grateful to yoga, aerial arts, and the flying trapeze(!) as they helped her embody grief with strength, grace, and artistry. She loves the occasional opportunity to teach yoga or encourage a new aerialist through their first challenging trick.

Sherry and her husband, Rob, reside in Minneapolis where they spend much of their time taking their children to music rehearsals and cleaning clay out of the rug.

www.sherrywalling.com

www.ZenFounder.com

About Sounds True

SOUNDS TRUE IS a multimedia publisher whose mission is to inspire and support personal transformation and spiritual awakening. Founded in 1985 and located in Boulder, Colorado, we work with many of the leading spiritual teachers, thinkers, healers, and visionary artists of our time. We strive with every title to preserve the essential "living wisdom" of the author or artist. It is our goal to create products that not only provide information to a reader or listener but also embody the quality of a wisdom transmission.

For those seeking genuine transformation, Sounds True is your trusted partner. At SoundsTrue.com you will find a wealth of free resources to support your journey, including exclusive weekly audio interviews, free downloads, interactive learning tools, and other special savings on all our titles.

To learn more, please visit SoundsTrue.com/freegifts or call us toll-free at 800.333.9185.